THE LIFE AND DEATH OF

ADOLF
HITLER

THE LIFE AND DEATH OF

ADOLF HITLER

BY JAMES CROSS GIBLIN

CLARION BOOKS
New York

Clarion Books
a Houghton Mifflin Company imprint
215 Park Avenue South, New York, NY 10003
Copyright © 2002 by James Cross Giblin

The type was set in 12-point Sabon.
Book design by Carol Goldenberg.
Maps on pages 103 and 165 by Victor Salvucci.

Printed in the USA

LIBRARY OF CONGRESS CATALOGING-IN-PUBLICATION DATA

Giblin, James.
The life and death of Adolf Hitler / by James Cross Giblin.
p.   cm.
Includes bibliographical references and index.
ISBN 0-395-90371-8
1. Hitler, Adolf, 1889-1945. 2. Heads of state—Germany—Biography.
3. National socialism. 4. Germany—History—1918–1933.
5. Germany—History—1933–1945. I. Title.

DD247.H5 G49 2002
943086'092—dc21
[B]   2001047091

VB 10 9 8 7 6 5 4 3 2 1

FRONTISPIECE:
Hitler addressing the Reichstag on September 1, 1939. *The Library of Congress.*

TO THE MEMORY OF DOROTHY BRILEY

ACKNOWLEDGMENTS

Thanks to the following who provided research material or illustrations for the book: Joan Carroll, AP/Wide World Photos; Corbis Images; Eric A. Kimmel; The Library of Congress, Prints and Photographs Division; Murray Liebman; Davida N. List; The National Archives; The New York Public Library

Special thanks to Renée Cafiero for her meticulous copyediting, and to Michael L. Cooper for his help with the picture research in Washington.

This poster reads across the top: "Youth serves the Führer." The bottom line reads: "All ten-year-olds into HJ [*Hitlerjugend*]." *The Library of Congress*

CONTENTS

Adolf Hitler in the late 1920s. *The Library of Congress*

1 · THE MOST DANGEROUS DICTATOR

THERE ARE NO MEMORIALS to Adolf Hitler in Germany, the country he ruled with an iron hand from 1933 to 1945. Nor do visitors flock to his grave, for no one knows where his remains are buried—or if they were buried at all. Perhaps his ashes, like his skull, remain locked away in an archive in Russia. Or perhaps they were scattered to the winds years ago at some unknown location in eastern Europe.

The mystery surrounding Hitler's remains has been maintained deliberately. In the years immediately after World War II, it was feared that die-hard followers of the German leader might flock to his gravesite to venerate him. At the same time, opponents of Hitler and everything he stood for were sure to stage protests at the site. To avoid conflict and controversy, the Russians, who discovered Hitler's remains at the end of the war, decided to keep their whereabouts a secret.

It was probably a wise move. Even today, almost sixty years after his death, Adolf Hitler remains a figure who inspires the anger and hatred of millions. Some younger people may not know exactly who he was, or the terrible crimes he committed. But their parents and grandparents and great-grandparents are sure to remember them. For Hitler's murderous actions left their mark, in one way or another, on everyone who lived in the latter two-thirds of the twentieth century.

How can one begin to understand a man like Adolf Hitler? Perhaps the best way to start is with the fact that he was a dictator—a leader with absolute power and authority over the people he ruled. Hitler was by no means the first such leader. The idea of a dictator originated over two thousand years ago in ancient Rome, where the great general Julius Caesar had himself named "Dictator for Life." The Romans abolished the position after Caesar was assassinated in 44 B.C., and the word fell into disuse.

The concept of an all-powerful ruler did not die out, however. Through the centuries that followed, kings, queens, emperors, and czars—relatively benevolent ones such as Russia's Peter the Great, and completely self-centered ones such as France's Louis XIV—exerted complete control over their subjects. Then, starting in the late 1700s in America and France, the people of many nations revolted against their royal rulers and established new forms of democratic government in their place.

The new democracies were often weak at the start, and the winds of change that blew through the world in the late nineteenth and early twentieth centuries did little to strengthen them. A steady parade of wars and revolutions led to inflation, high unemployment, and poverty in many countries, including Germany. These unsettled conditions proved to be a fertile breeding ground for a new type of dictator. From Europe to Asia to Latin America, leaders like Hitler arose claiming they could solve all of their nations' problems if they were given the power to do so.

In most instances, the influence of the new dictators did not extend beyond the borders of their own countries. But some harbored grander ambitions. In Italy, Benito Mussolini envisioned a new Roman Empire. In Russia, Vladimir Ilyich Lenin and Joseph Stalin strove to build a Communist society that would serve as a launching pad for a worldwide revolution. But the most dangerous—and ultimately the most destructive—twentieth-century dictator was Adolf Hitler.

After suppressing all internal opposition to his regime, Hitler pursued an aggressive foreign policy aimed at bringing much of central and eastern Europe under German control. His invasion of Poland in 1939 set off the Second World War, a conflict that spread around the globe and claimed the lives of more than 50 million people. But Hitler's crimes against humanity did not end there. In Germany and the countries it seized, he launched a campaign to exterminate entire groups of people he deemed "inferior." These included gypsies, homosexuals, and most of all the Jews, 6 million of whom would die before Hitler's reign of terror came to an end.

What sort of man could plan and carry out such horrendous schemes? How was he able to win support for his deadly ventures? And why did no one try to stop him until it was almost too late? Those are the questions for which countless biographers, historians, and psychologists have sought answers in the years since Hitler's death. They are also the questions this book will explore.

2·YOUNG ADOLF

IT'S HARD TO FIND HINTS in the young Adolf Hitler of the cruel dictator he was to become. In fact, his childhood seems to have been quite normal for a boy of his time. He was born on April 20, 1889, in the small Austrian town of Braunau at the border between Austria and Germany. Christened Adolphus Hitler, he was his parents' fourth child, and the first to live beyond the age of two.

The Hitler family led a comfortable, middle-class existence. Adolf's father, Alois, was a respected Austrian customs official, responsible for the inspection of people and goods crossing the border to and from Germany. His mother, Klara, was a former housemaid whom her doctor described as "simple, modest, and kindly."

Klara Hitler doted on Adolf but also found time for his half-brother and half-sister, Alois, Jr., and Angela, who lived with the family. They were Alois Hitler's children by a previous marriage. Completing the household was Adolf's aunt Johanna, his mother's younger sister. Johanna was a hunchback whose affliction made her bitter and bad-tempered. But she always had a soft spot for her nephew.

As Adolf grew up, he enjoyed playing cops and robbers with his friends in the woods and fields around their homes. Along with thousands of other German-speaking youngsters, he devoured the adventure novels of Karl May, who wrote rousing tales of the Wild West although he had never been to America. But Adolf was a mediocre student at best. One of his teachers remembered him as "a thin, pale youth who lacked application, did not make full use of his talents, and was unable to accommodate himself to school discipline."

By then Adolf had a little brother, Edmund, born in 1894, and a sister,

Adolf Hitler as a baby. *The National Archives*

Paula, born in 1896. His father had retired in 1895 after forty years of loyal service to the Austro-Hungarian Empire, and the family was living on his generous pension in a small farming community not far from the Austrian city of Linz. With five children, including a baby, crowded into the house, Alois Hitler frequently lost his temper and beat his sons with a whip if they did something to offend him. The older boy, Alois, Jr., was the more frequent target of his father's rage, but sometimes Adolf was beaten, too, if he brought home a poor report card.

Alois, Jr., resented his younger half-brother. Years later he said of Adolf, "He was quick to anger from childhood onward and would not listen to anyone. He would get the craziest notions and get away with them. And my stepmother always took his part." At fourteen, Alois, Jr., had finally had enough. He ran away from home and did not return during his father's lifetime.

After Alois, Jr., left, Adolf felt the brunt of his father's temper. He had read in one of Karl May's novels that a hero could prove his courage by

Painting of Alois Hitler, Adolf's father.
The Library of Congress

Klara Hitler, Adolf's mother.
The Library of Congress

showing no pain. "I then resolved never to cry when my father whipped me," he told a friend. "A few days later I had the opportunity of putting my will to the test. My mother, frightened, took refuge in front of the door. As for me, I counted silently the blows of the stick which lashed my buttocks." After that, according to Adolf, his father never beat him again.

In 1900, when Adolf was about to finish primary school, his younger brother, Edmund, died of measles. This family tragedy heightened the conflict between Adolf and his father. Alois was a patriotic Austrian who was determined that Adolf follow in his footsteps and prepare for a career in the Empire civil service. Young Adolf admired Germany and Otto von Bismarck, the leader who had built it into a great power. He had absolutely no interest in becoming an Austrian civil servant. "I yawned and grew sick to my stomach at the thought of sitting in an office, deprived of my liberty; ceasing to be master of my own time," he wrote in his autobiography, *Mein Kampf* (My Struggle).

What Adolf really wanted was to become an artist. He enjoyed drawing and had already shown some talent at it. But he knew what the reaction would be if he told his father of his ambition: "An artist, no, never as long as I live!" he could imagine the man saying.

Still, some decision had to be made about Adolf's future education. After graduating from primary school, he could enroll in a *Gymnasium,* the type of secondary school that emphasized language and literature and prepared a student for entrance to a university. Or he could attend a *Realschule,* the kind that stressed scientific and technical studies. Being a practical man, Alois favored the latter. Adolf agreed to his father's plan once he learned that *Realschule*s also offered classes in drawing.

The sixth-grade class of the Linz Realschule poses with their teacher in June 1901. Twelve-year-old Adolf Hitler is the last one on the right in the back row.
The Library of Congress

The young Hitler did well in those classes but earned less-than-average grades in history and geography and failed mathematics and French. "I thought that once my father saw how little progress I was making at the *Realschule,* he would let me devote myself to my dream [of being an artist], whether he liked it or not," Adolf wrote.

What his father thought would soon cease to matter. On January 3, 1903, Alois Hitler stopped by the local inn for his morning glass of wine, complained of not feeling well, and dropped dead at his table. He was sixty-six. In its obituary notice, a Linz newspaper commented, "The sharp word that fell occasionally from his lips could not belie the warm heart that beat beneath the rough exterior."

After his father's death, Adolf continued his studies at several different *Realschule*s, passing some subjects but failing others. Then, in the summer of 1905, while vacationing with his mother and sister, Paula, in the countryside, he fell ill with a lung infection. Perhaps it was serious, perhaps not. In any case, he used it as an excuse not to return to the *Realschule* in the fall. His mother accepted his decision, and so, at the age of sixteen, Adolf Hitler ended his formal education.

Klara Hitler was now living comfortably with Paula and Aunt Johanna in an apartment in the center of Linz. Her stepdaughter, Angela, had left home following her marriage to a tax collector, Leo Raubal. Adolf moved in with his mother, and for the next two years he spent his days enjoying all the cultural activities Linz had to offer. He filled sketchbooks with drawings, went to museums, plays, and operas, and daydreamed of his future life as a great artist. And one night at the opera, he met a young man with similar dreams, August Kubizek. The two soon became inseparable friends.

August, called Gustl, the son of an upholsterer, helped his father in his shop but really wanted to pursue a career in music. Unlike Hitler, he worked hard to fulfill his ambition. Already he had mastered the violin, viola, and trumpet, and now he was studying music theory. Quiet by nature, August was awed by Hitler's way with words. After attending an opera, the two friends, dressed in their best clothes, would stroll through the darkened streets of Linz before going home. As they walked, Adolf would twirl his ivory-handled cane as he discussed every aspect of the performance they had just seen, while August listened admiringly.

Adolf rarely talked about himself, but one time August dared to ask

Profile of Hitler at age sixteen, drawn by a classmate in Linz.
The National Archives

him if he worked. "Of course not!" was Hitler's reply. He had no time, he said, for some dreary "bread-and-butter job."

Nor did Adolf talk about girls, except on one occasion when he pointed out a young woman in a crowd on Linz's main street. Her name was Stephanie Jansten, Hitler said, adding that she lived not far from him. August turned to look at the girl, noting that she was tall and slim, with thick, fair hair swept up into a coil on top of her head. "You must know that I'm in love with her!" Adolf said, gripping his friend's arm. But he admitted that he had never said a word to her, never even approached her, in fact.

In the spring of 1906, Adolf got his mother to fund his first trip to the great city of Vienna, 118 miles east of Linz. He stayed with relatives and spent two weeks exploring the capital of the Austro-Hungarian Empire, then as now a major center of art, architecture, and music. "Tomorrow I go to the opera to see Wagner's *Tristan,*" he wrote on a postcard to August, "the day after to *The Flying Dutchman.*" He wasn't impressed by Vienna's Royal Opera House. "Only when the mighty waves of sound roll through space . . . does one feel nobility and forget the gold and velvet with which the interior is overloaded," he wrote August on another card. But he was tremendously impressed by the grandeur of Vienna's palaces and public buildings.

Adolf returned to Linz more determined than ever to devote his life to art and architecture. He led August on long walking tours of the city, during which he praised one building and criticized the next. Then he would tell his friend in great detail how he himself would redesign the buildings that offended him. "He gave his whole self to his imaginary building plans," August said, "and was completely carried away by them."

Harsh reality soon brought Adolf down to earth. In January 1907, his mother was diagnosed with breast cancer. Her physician, Dr. Edward Bloch, told Adolf and his sister that an operation might help, but he was not too hopeful. Later, the doctor remembered that tears flowed from Adolf's eyes when he heard the news. "'Did his mother have no chance?' he asked. Only then," the doctor wrote, "did I recognize the magnitude of the attachment that existed between mother and son."

The family decided to risk the operation, and Klara seemed to make a good recovery. Aunt Johanna took over many of her household duties, and Adolf resumed his usual ways. He stayed at home most of the day, reading, painting watercolors, and making architectural sketches. In the evening he would join his friend August for a night at the theater or the opera.

Hitler was now eighteen and had yet to work a day in his life. Some of his relatives felt it was long past time that he get a job. One suggested that he apply at the post office. Another found a baker who said he would take Adolf on as an apprentice. But the youth continued to insist that he was going to be a great artist one day. In the summer of 1907, he persuaded his mother to give him a loan so that he could move to Vienna. He had decided he wanted to study at the city's renowned Academy of Fine Arts, which held its entrance examination in October. If he didn't apply now, he would have to wait another year.

Klara gave in to her son's pleas, even though she hated the thought of Adolf leaving home. He took the train to Vienna in late September and settled into a rented room near the city center. On the day of the examination, armed with a stack of sample drawings, he presented himself at the Academy along with 112 other applicants. Thirty-three were rejected following an initial screening, but Adolf was invited to take a second, more difficult test in which the applicants had to produce a detailed drawing on a specified theme. Only twenty-eight applicants passed this test—and Adolf was not one of them. "Test drawing unsatisfactory," the judges said.

Adolf was devastated. "I was so convinced that I would be successful that when I received my rejection, it struck me as a bolt from the blue," he wrote in his autobiography. How could he tell his mother and August that he had failed, after boasting so often that he was destined to be a great artist? The answer was that he didn't. He stayed on in Vienna but kept the rejection a secret from everyone he knew in Linz.

To add to his woes, Adolf received word that his mother's cancer had returned and her condition was worsening. He hurried home to Linz, only to be told by Dr. Bloch that the situation was hopeless. In the days that followed, Adolf surprised everyone by devoting himself entirely to his mother's care. According to his friend August, he spoke "not a cross or impatient word" and never once insisted on having his own way. In those weeks, August said, "Adolf lived only for his mother."

His loving care could not save her, though. In the early-morning hours of December 21, 1907, Klara Hitler died as quietly as she had lived. Later that day, Dr. Bloch came to the Hitler home to sign the death certificate. He found Adolf, his face pale and drawn, sitting beside his mother's body. On a sketchpad nearby was a drawing he had made of her face, peaceful and relaxed in death.

"I had honored my father," Adolf would write later, "but my mother I had loved." As he mourned her, the young Hitler must have wondered what he would do next. First the Academy of Fine Arts had rejected him, and now he had lost the person who had meant more to him than anyone else in life.

3 · HOMELESS IN VIENNA

AFTER HELPING TO SETTLE his mother's estate, Adolf made plans to return to Vienna. He estimated that his share of the estate would enable him to live in the city without working for at least a year.

Adolf persuaded his friend August to come with him and study music, despite his family's objections. The two young men took rooms in a boarding house, and within a few days August had registered at Vienna's Conservatory of Music and passed its rigorous entrance examination. "I had no idea I had such a clever friend," was Adolf's only comment, and he showed no interest in August's progress at the Conservatory in the weeks that followed.

Adolf had never told August that he himself had failed the entrance examination at the Academy of Fine Arts. But one day the truth came out. After launching a fierce attack on the Academy's professors, calling them "a lot of old-fashioned, fossilized civil servants," Hitler admitted that they had turned him down the fall before. August tried to console him, but Adolf brushed aside his attempt at sympathy and changed the subject.

Despite their limited finances, the two young men frequently went to concerts and to the opera, even if it meant skipping a meal or two. Hitler was a devoted fan of the German composer Richard Wagner. His passionate music had the power to transport Adolf into a mystical dream world where humans had the strength of gods. Hitler's favorite Wagnerian opera was *Lohengrin,* about a heroic German knight. He and August attended no fewer than ten performances of *Lohengrin* during the winter of 1908.

Vienna in the early years of the twentieth century was a freewheeling city where every sort of sexual activity flourished. Hitler was fascinated by the notorious district where prostitutes patrolled the streets or waited for customers behind lighted windows. But he was also repelled by it, linking prostitution with venereal disease and lecturing August on the need to maintain one's sexual purity at all costs. From the available evidence, both young men did so, no matter what temptations may have presented themselves along the way.

After finishing his classes with honors and conducting the end-of-semester concert, August went home to Linz to spend the summer of 1908 with his parents. Adolf stayed on in Vienna in his stifling room, working on a new batch of architectural drawings. He had decided to try again for admission to the Academy of Fine Arts, and he would need to submit examples of his recent work.

Without telling August or anyone else, Adolf applied once more to the Academy in mid-September—and once more he was rejected. This time the judges had such a low opinion of his sample drawings that he wasn't asked to take the second part of the examination. This rejection was a more crushing blow to Adolf than the first had been. But he couldn't afford to dwell on it, for he had an even more immediate problem to deal with: His money was running out.

He gave up his room in the boarding house and took a smaller, cheaper one in a rundown house overlooking the railroad yards. August was due back from Linz any day, but Adolf didn't leave a note telling his friend where he had gone. He was probably too embarrassed by his second failure at the Academy and his lack of money.

For the next five years, Adolf Hitler led the life of a reclusive nomad in Vienna. His friend August heard nothing from him, and he was rarely in contact with his family in Linz. With the money from his mother's estate gone, and only a tiny monthly "orphan's pension" coming in, he was forced to move into smaller and smaller rooms. Eventually he couldn't afford even the smallest cubbyhole and had to take to the streets. Wrapped in his overcoat, he slept at night in one or another of Vienna's parks. The next morning he lined up outside a Catholic convent, where the nuns distributed soup and bread to the homeless.

When cold weather came, he trudged across the city to a shelter he had heard about. There he was assigned a bed in the men's dormitory, his bug-infested clothes were disinfected, and he himself enjoyed a long, warm shower—his first bath in months. Soon after his arrival at the shelter, Hitler was befriended by a fellow resident, Reinhold Hanisch. The two of them made a little money by shoveling snow in front of fancy hotels and carrying luggage for passengers at the main railroad station.

Hitler told Hanisch that he was an artist but had been forced to sell his painting materials when he was living in the streets. This gave Hanisch an idea; he persuaded Adolf to write his aunt Johanna for money to buy new brushes and paints. There was a good market, Hanisch said, for original postcard paintings of Viennese landmarks. Once Adolf had the necessary materials, he could paint the scenes, and Hanisch would sell them in the city's hotels and taverns.

With part of the money Aunt Johanna sent him, Adolf moved to a more comfortable men's hostel. Each resident of the hostel had his own tiny room, and there was a common room where Adolf could paint at one of the tables. Hanisch soon joined him at the hostel, and together they developed a profitable business. Adolf alternated postcard scenes with larger watercolors, and Hanisch was able to sell them all. But when Hanisch pressed him to produce more paintings, Adolf rebelled. He wanted time for other activities and broke off his partnership with Hanisch.

Continuing on his own, Adolf painted fewer pictures but sold almost all of them through various dealers. He also engaged in spirited political discussions with other residents in the hostel's common room. A fierceness would come into his voice when he denounced the corruption he saw all around him in Vienna. He was particularly scornful of the left-leaning Social Democratic Party. One day he got into a fight with two burly workers, whom he had called "idiots" when they said they were members of a Social Democratic labor organization. The workers left him with bruises and a swollen jaw.

During this period, Hitler read many right-wing newspapers and magazines that linked the Social Democrats with the Jews. Later, he would write in his autobiography that the roots of his lifelong hatred of the Jews were planted during these years in Vienna. He gradually became aware, he said, of what he saw as their evil influence on the city's political, economic, and cultural life. If this was true, Adolf must have kept his feelings to himself. He enjoyed the companionship of several Jewish friends during his stay at the hostel, and had nothing but praise for a Jewish art dealer, Jacob Altenberg, who sold many of his paintings.

Detail of a watercolor by Hitler. This is one of the postcard-type scenes he painted for a living during his stay in Munich. *The Library of Congress*

In April 1913, Adolf received his share of his father's estate, which he had not been able to claim until his twenty-fourth birthday. With this money in hand, he decided to move to Germany, whose literature and art he loved and where he had long wanted to live. He rented a room in the great city of Munich, capital of Bavaria, a southern German state that borders on Austria. There he began to paint street scenes much like those he had done in Vienna.

Munich in the early part of the twentieth century was one of the major world centers of modern art, the home of innovative painters like Wassily Kandinsky and Paul Klee. But Hitler showed no interest whatsoever in modernism. What impressed him instead were Munich's grand boulevards, its art museums filled with fine old master paintings, its magnificent palaces and public buildings. Adolf strolled the city's streets with his sketchbook, drawings scenes that he would later paint. In his autobiography, he would call this period "the happiest and by far the most contented of my life."

His happy mood did not last long. In January 1914, he received a summons to report in his hometown of Linz for duty in the Austrian army. The last thing Adolf wanted at this point was to return to Austria and serve in its armed forces. He managed to have the city where he reported changed to Salzburg, an Austrian city closer to Munich. When he appeared there on February 5, his rundown appearance had the desired effect on the recruiters, who declared him "unfit for combat and auxiliary duties, too weak. Unable to bear arms."

Adolf reacted in an entirely different way when word came later that year that the heir to the Austro-Hungarian throne, Archduke Franz Ferdinand, had been assassinated by a young Serbian terrorist. At the urging

Crowd gathered in a Munich square in August 1914 cheers the news that war has been declared. Hitler is singled out in the circled closeup. *Corbis/Bettman*

of its ally, Germany, Austria declared war on Serbia on July 28. Russia mobilized its army to come to the aid of *its* ally, Serbia. The leader of Germany, Kaiser Wilhelm II, issued an ultimatum to the Russians, demanding that they cease the mobilization by noon of the following day or face the consequences. Russia did not respond, and so at five P.M. on August 1, 1914, Germany mobilized its army against the Russians. The conflict that would become known as World War I had begun.

A large crowd that had gathered in one of Munich's main squares cheered when they heard the news. Adolf Hitler, who stood near the front of the throng, was overjoyed. His native Austria had joined forces with his adopted country, Germany, to wage war against Russia and Serbia. It made him proud to be a resident of Germany. He wrote in *Mein Kampf*: "I am not ashamed to say that, overcome with rapturous enthusiasm, I fell to my knees and thanked Heaven . . . for granting me the good fortune of being allowed to live at this time." Two days later, on August 3, he requested permission to enlist in the Bavarian army.

His appeal must have been eloquent, for he received a reply the very next day. "With trembling hands I opened the document," he wrote. "My request had been approved, and I was summoned to report to a Bavarian regiment. My joy and gratitude knew no bounds. A few days later I was wearing the tunic [uniform] I was not to doff until nearly six years later."

Besides giving him tremendous emotional satisfaction, his enlistment in the army solved several of Hitler's most pressing problems. He might face dangers in battle, but meanwhile he would be guaranteed food and shelter and would not have to worry about making an uncertain living with his paintings. More important, for the first time in his life, he would have a definite purpose—to fight for Germany, the nation he had passionately admired since he was a boy.

4 · CORPORAL HITLER

AFTER BASIC TRAINING in a camp near Munich, Adolf and his fellow recruits boarded a train for the front on October 20, 1914. By then France and England had joined Russia in the war against Germany and Austria, and fighting in the west was centered near the city of Ypres in Belgium.

On arrival in Belgium, Hitler's company was assigned to relieve an exhausted unit on the frontline. As they advanced, the British began firing shells in their direction. "Now the first shrapnel hisses over us and explodes at the edge of the forest, splintering trees as if they were straws," Adolf wrote later to an acquaintance in Munich.

"Four times we advance and have to go back," he continued. "From my whole batch only one remains, beside me; finally he also falls. A shot tears off my right coat sleeve, but like a miracle I remain safe and alive. At 2 o'clock we finally go forward for the fifth time, and this time we occupy the edge of the forest and the farms."

As the German attack continued, Adolf was made a dispatch carrier for the regiment. He risked his life on many occasions, delivering messages under fire from one segment of the front to another. After the offensive to take Ypres failed, the German and English armies dug themselves in opposite each other and engaged in what was known as trench warfare. Except for an occasional skirmish, the battle lines remained frozen for long periods of time. During this lull in the fighting, Adolf received an Iron Cross, Second Class, for his bravery as a dispatch carrier and runner. "It was the happiest day of my life," he wrote his Munich landlord. "Unfortunately, my comrades who also earned it are mostly dead." Hitler was promoted at this time from private to corporal.

His fellow soldiers had nothing but admiration for Adolf's courage and skill as a runner. He could crawl unseen over the battle-scarred earth like one of the Indian scouts in the Western stories he had devoured as a youngster. But sometimes, he seemed almost too eager to do his duty. When the fighting intensified in 1915, he would leap out of his bunk as soon as the English artillery barrage started at dawn. Eager for action, he would grab his rifle and stride up and down in the trench, rousing all the soldiers who were still asleep.

Although few of his comrades disliked Adolf, many of them thought him strange. He neither smoked nor drank, and he showed no interest in girls. When the conversation of his fellow soldiers turned to their sexual conquests, Adolf would retreat to a corner of the dugout to read a book or draw in his sketchbook. Nor did he talk much about family or friends, and when mail was distributed, he rarely got any letters. The one

Corporal Adolf Hitler (bottom left), his mustache larger than usual, poses with a group of his fellow soldiers during a quiet moment at the front in 1916.
The National Archives

creature he seemed to care about was his dog, a little white terrier who had strayed into the German trenches one day. He named the dog Fuchsl (Foxy), taught him how to do tricks, and delighted in the affection the animal showered on him.

In the summer of 1916, Adolf's regiment moved south to join in the crucial battle taking place along the Somme River in France. Time and again Adolf was sent out on dangerous missions under heavy enemy fire, and time and again he returned safely. Then one night in October, his luck ran out. He was sleeping sitting up with his fellow messengers in a narrow tunnel when a shell exploded nearby. The blast shook up the messengers and a piece of shrapnel cut into Hitler's thigh.

He wanted to stay with his regiment, but the lieutenant in charge decided he should go to a field hospital for treatment. From there he was sent back to Germany to recuperate in a military hospital near Berlin. As soon as he could walk again, he got a pass to spend the weekend in the city. He had never been in the German capital and was eager to see its art museums and grand public buildings. But he was not prepared for the mood of depression and defeatism that hung over the city like a fog. He was outraged when he heard men boasting how they had managed to avoid military service, and speakers in the parks telling crowds of onlookers that Germany was bound to lose the war.

After two months in the military hospital, Hitler was declared fit for duty again and told to report to a battalion stationed in Munich. If he had been disillusioned by what he'd seen in Berlin, he was appalled by the conditions he found in Munich. Morale was terrible—"anger, discontent, cursing wherever you went!" he wrote later. The people he encountered were obviously miserable. Grocery stores had little to sell, and evidence of poverty was everywhere. What had happened to the spirit of enthusiasm with which Munich had greeted the start of the war nearly three years earlier?

As Hitler walked the city's streets, he sought an explanation for the steep decline in patriotic spirit. He soon decided he'd found the answer: the Jews. "The offices were filled with Jews," he wrote in *Mein Kampf*. "Nearly every clerk was a Jew, and nearly every Jew was a clerk. I was amazed at this plethora of warriors of the chosen people and could not help but compare them with their rare representatives at the front."

(Which was not an accurate observation: Many Jews served with distinction in the German army in the First World War.)

"As regards economic life, things were even worse," Hitler went on. "Here the Jewish people had become really 'indispensable.' The spider was beginning to suck the blood out of the people's pores. Through the war corporations, they had found an instrument with which, little by little, to finish off the national economy." Again, Hitler's conclusions were far from the truth, but unfortunately they were shared by many Germans. Like him, they were looking for a scapegoat whom they could blame for the military stalemate at the front and the steady decline in living conditions at home.

Disgusted with the young recruits in the Munich battalion, who showed no respect for veteran soldiers like himself, Hitler applied for permission to rejoin his old regiment in France. His request was granted, and on March 1, 1917, he was welcomed back warmly by his comrades. His dog, Fuchsl, was especially excited by Hitler's return. "He hurled himself on me in a frenzy," Adolf wrote, glad to be back in the place where he felt most at home: his army regiment.

Hitler's sense of satisfaction would not last long, however. The United States entered the war in April 1917, and American troops soon reinforced the British and French forces on the western front. Hitler's regiment was transferred to Belgium to participate in another onslaught on the city of Ypres. The fighting there was fiercer than ever as the German soldiers faced two new and deadly weapons: armored tanks on the ground and poison gas in the air. Sometimes Adolf and his comrades had to wear their uncomfortable gas masks for twenty-four hours straight.

In August, just as Hitler's regiment was about to go on leave, Adolf suffered two losses. Someone stole the leather case in which he kept his sketches and watercolors. At the same time, his beloved dog disappeared. "I was desperate," Adolf said. Fuchsl meant more to him than his sketches—more than any of the comrades he had seen die at the front. He hunted everywhere for the animal, but had to give up the search when his regiment marched on.

The war took a new turn in November 1917, when Communist revolutionaries, led by Vladimir Ilyich Lenin, overthrew the government of Russia. One of the first acts of the new Communist regime was to pro-

German soldiers on alert in a frontline trench in France in 1917.
The Library of Congress

pose an armistice in the fighting with Germany, and the two countries signed a peace treaty in March 1918. But Russia's departure from the war did not significantly ease the situation on the western front or in Germany itself. Adolf and his comrades had to put up with shorter rations, and some soldiers were forced to eat cats, dogs, and even rats. There was almost no milk to be had in German cities, and people ate bread made of sawdust and potato peelings.

Inspired by the revolution in Russia, workers in Germany had gone on strike in January 1918, demanding increased food rations and the start of negotiations to end the war. The workers were forced back to work within a week, but a spirit of revolt had been aroused in Berlin and other German cities. Meanwhile, at the front in France, many soldiers felt they had been betrayed by their own people. "What was the army fighting for if the homeland itself no longer wanted victory?" Hitler wrote later. "For whom the immense sacrifices and privations? The soldier is expected to fight for victory, and the homeland goes on strike against it!"

On August 4, 1918, Adolf received his second Iron Cross—this one in the First Class category. The citation said it was for bravery shown in delivering an important dispatch from command headquarters to the frontline, following a breakdown in telephone communications and under heavy enemy fire. But even as he was accepting the award, the last major German offensive of the war was collapsing in the face of a determined counterattack by the Allies—Britain, France, and the United States. In the previous four months alone, the Germans had lost almost 800,000 soldiers, and their reserves of both men and supplies were seriously depleted.

Still they fought on. By the end of September, Adolf's regiment had retreated to Belgium, where it was under assault from British troops employing the dreaded mustard gas as a weapon. On the night of October 13–14, Hitler himself fell victim to it. "On a hill south of Wervik, we came into several hours of drumfire with gas shells which continued all night," he wrote. "As early as midnight, a number of us passed out, a few of our comrades forever. Toward morning I, too, was seized with pain which grew worse with every quarter hour, and at seven in the morning I stumbled and tottered back with burning eyes, taking with me my last report of the War. A few hours later, my eyes had turned into glowing coals; it had grown dark around me."

It had grown dark for Germany, too. As Hitler was being treated for his temporary blindness, first in Belgium and then at a military hospital in Germany, the Kaiser and his generals were taking the first steps to end the war. Germany had been defeated, and the country was collapsing into chaos.

5 · THE POWER OF SPEECH

ALL GERMANY WAS IN TURMOIL. Revolutionaries seized power in the cities of Munich, Hanover, and Cologne. One regional German government after another was toppled by workers' and soldiers' councils. At last, on November 9, 1918, Kaiser Wilhelm was forced to abdicate, and the German Empire came to an end. Two days later, the new Social Democratic government signed an armistice agreement with the victorious Allies. The First World War was over.

Adolf Hitler, recuperating in a military hospital, could not see to read the newspapers. Consequently, he knew little of what was going on until a pastor came to the hospital and sorrowfully informed the patients that the monarchy had been replaced by a republic, and that the war had been lost.

Hitler reacted violently to this news. "It became impossible for me to sit still one minute more," he wrote in *Mein Kampf*. "Again everything went black before my eyes; I tottered and groped my way back to the dormitory, threw myself on my bunk, and dug my burning head into my blanket and pillow.

"Since the day when I had stood at my mother's grave, I had not wept. . . . But now I could not help it. . . . So it had all been in vain. . . . Did all this happen only so that a gang of wretched criminals could lay hands on the Fatherland? . . . What was all the pain in my eyes compared to this misery?"

The imperial German government that Hitler had supported so enthusiastically had suddenly vanished. He felt betrayed—and angry. It was at this point, he wrote later, that he made the decision that would change his life, and the lives of hundreds of millions of others. "I, for my part, decided to go into politics," he said.

At the end of November, his vision restored, Adolf was discharged from the hospital and told to report for duty to a military battalion in Munich. There he met other soldiers who shared his distress at what had happened to their beloved country. They sympathized with a right-wing group known as the Free Corps, veterans of the frontline fighting who blamed the Jews and the Communists for Germany's defeat. Several of the men, including Adolf, volunteered to serve as guards at a prisoner-of-war camp near Munich.

Meanwhile, Germany continued to be racked by political unrest. In Berlin, members of the Free Corps clashed with the Communists, who were trying to seize power in the city from the Social Democrats. Only the arrival of Free Corps units from other parts of Germany enabled the government to regain control. Soon afterward, the first national elections of the new republic were held, and moderates won the majority of seats in the Reichstag, Germany's parliament. But the political scene had not really quieted down, for the Free Corps, the Communists, and other extremist groups were still feverishly organizing behind the scenes. Because of the continuing unrest in Berlin, the recently elected Reichstag met in the university town of Weimar. As a result, the new German government came to be known as the Weimar Republic.

The next target of the revolutionaries was Munich, where the city's Social Democratic government was overthrown by Communists in April 1919. The Communists' rule did not last long, however. The ousted Social Democrats joined forces with the Free Corps to retake the city. Outnumbered, the Communists put up little resistance as Free Corps members roamed through the city, subduing the few Communists who opposed them and arresting their leaders.

It's not clear what role, if any, Adolf Hitler played in the Munich revolution and its suppression. He had returned to duty in the city in February after the prisoner-of-war camp shut down, and in May he was given a new assignment. In the wake of the Munich turmoil, the army decided to indoctrinate the troops against the threat of Communism so that they would be prepared for any future takeover attempts. To do so, it needed well-informed instructors who knew the army and its ways. Hitler was one of those chosen for training as an instructor.

Adolf committed himself wholeheartedly to his classes in history, economics, and politics, which were held at Munich University. After graduating in August, he was assigned to teach a five-day course on the virtues of nationalism and the dangers of Communism to returning German prisoners of war. He threw himself into his lectures and discovered that he had the power to move an audience. His gifts did not go unnoticed by his superiors. One of them wrote in an evaluation, "Herr Hitler is a born people's speaker. . . . He clearly compels the attention of his listeners, and makes them think his way."

Adolf's newfound skill led to many speaking assignments in and around Munich. "I started out with the greatest enthusiasm and love," he wrote in *Mein Kampf*. "And I could boast of some success: in the course of my lectures I led many hundreds, indeed thousands, of comrades back to their people and Fatherland." Hitler also helped to investigate the activities of the fifty or so radical organizations that had sprung up recently in Munich. One of these was a small political group, the German Workers' Party, whose program was based on a combination of socialism, nationalism, and anti-Semitism.

Adolf felt an immediate rapport with this party, whose political goals were so similar to his own. After reading his report, Hitler's military superiors became interested in the party also. They were looking for workers' groups that would support the rebuilding of the German army, and the German Workers' Party seemed a likely candidate. His superiors ordered Adolf to join the party and help to build it up, and he was happy to oblige. Given his feelings, he would probably have joined it on his own.

Thus began Adolf Hitler's active political career. Spearheaded by his abilities as an orator, the German Workers' Party grew within a few months from a handful of men meeting in the back room of a shabby restaurant to an organization that attracted audiences of 2,000 and more. Hitler's speeches were based on the new party program that he had helped to write. It called for the union of all German-speaking peoples in one great realm, or Reich; the establishment of new colonies abroad; the creation of a strong people's army; and a "ruthless battle" against criminals to insure law and order throughout the country.

Hitler's audiences cheered when he demanded that the Versailles Treaty be revoked. Signed at the French town of Versailles in June 1919, the Treaty formally ended the First World War. It placed the entire responsibility for starting the war on Germany and its allies, and it imposed

Hitler discovers he has the power to excite crowds when he addresses rallies of the newly formed German Workers' Party. *The Library of Congress*

heavy reparation payments on Germany. Some of the payments were to be in kind—such as coal, steel, ships. For example, Germany had to turn over 43 million tons of coal yearly, to be divided among France, Belgium, and Italy. Other reparations were to be in cash, amounting to a total of $32 billion.

Germany also suffered a major loss of territory as a result of the Treaty. The regions of Alsace and Lorraine, which Germany had acquired in 1871 at the end of the Franco-Prussian War, were returned to France. In addition, Germany lost its colonies in Africa, and much of the state of East Prussia was awarded to Poland. The Saar region in Germany, with its many coal mines, was placed under French administration for fifteen years; the heavily industrialized Rhineland was to be occupied by the Allies for an equal period. The German army was reduced to a maximum of 100,000 men; the German navy was also reduced.

In drafting the Versailles Treaty, the Allies wanted to punish Germany so severely that it would never again contemplate launching a major war in Europe. But the Treaty aroused such tremendous resentment in Germany, and created such painful hardships for the German people, that many observers felt it was counterproductive. Not the least of its negative effects was the opportunity that it offered groups like the Communists, the Free Corps, and the German Workers' Party to generate support for their extremist policies.

The harshest words in Hitler's speeches were not aimed at the Versailles Treaty or the Communists, however. They were directed instead against the Jews, whom Hitler described as enemies of the German people. He demanded that the Jews be treated as aliens, that they be denied the right to hold any public office, and that they be deported from Germany if the nation found itself unable to feed its entire population.

After each point he made, Hitler would ask the audience if everyone understood and agreed with what he had said. Most of the crowd shouted their approval, but there were usually some hecklers, too. They were quickly silenced and ushered out of the hall by Hitler's soldier friends, who were scattered throughout the crowd. If any of the protesters dared to resist, the soldiers did not hesitate to use force to remove them.

A twenty-year-old law student, Hans Frank, gave his impressions of one of Hitler's early speeches. "The first thing you felt was there was a man who spoke honestly about what he believed," Frank said. At the end of the speech, when all the hecklers had been driven from the hall, the applause for Hitler was loud and long. By then young Frank was convinced that "if anyone could master the fate of Germany, Hitler was that man."

6 · LAUNCHING A REVOLUTION

IN MARCH 1920, Adolf Hitler received his army discharge after almost six years of military service, four of them on the frontlines. He had entered the army as a struggling artist who had little idea what he would do next. He left it as a rising star in German politics. With his demobilization pay of fifty marks in hand, he rented a small back room in a Munich boarding house and settled into his new life.

Through the rest of 1920, Adolf gave one impassioned speech after another to larger and larger crowds. He attracted important new members to the German Workers' Party, including army captain Ernst Röhm, whose troops helped keep order at Hitler's rallies. To make the Party sound more impressive, Hitler thought of a new name for it. It became the *Nationalsozialistische Deutsche Arbeiter Partei* (National Socialist German Workers' Party), but people soon shortened the name to just the Nazi Party.

Hitler also sought an emblem for the party flag that could compete with the hammer and sickle that appeared on the red banner of the Communists. A small-town German dentist came up with the winning entry: a black swastika against a red-and-white background. The swastika has a long history. It got its name from a word in the Sanskrit language, *svastika,* meaning well-being and good fortune, and the symbol is still used as a good-luck talisman by Hindus. For centuries a symbol similar to the swastika represented the wheel of the sun or the cycle of life to certain Native American tribes as well as European groups such as the Teutonic Knights. Now, as the emblem of the National Socialist Party, it would soon convey a much more sinister meaning.

By the beginning of 1921, membership in the Nazi Party had grown to

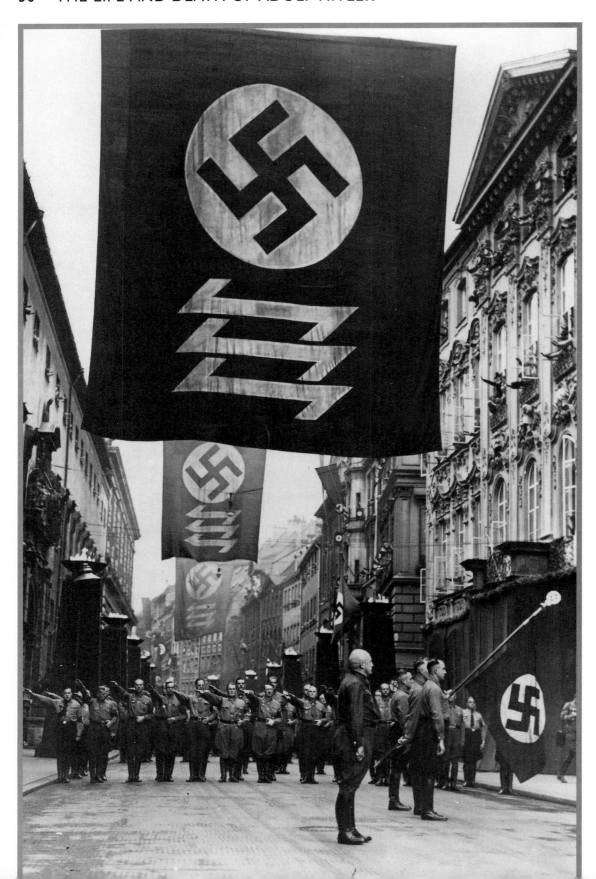

almost 3,000, thanks largely to Hitler's efforts. Its success attracted influential new allies: Otto and Gregor Strasser, prominent right-wing socialists, and General Erich von Ludendorff, one of Germany's top military leaders. To spread the party's word more widely, it acquired a newspaper, the *Völkischer Beobachter* (People's Observer), which was well known for its anti-Semitic editorial policy.

As the Party grew, it became more difficult to keep the various members in line. In July, Hitler asked to be made first party chairman and given dictatorial powers. "I make these demands," he said, "not because I am power hungry, but because without an iron leadership the party . . . will within a short time cease to be what it was supposed to be: a national socialist German Workers' Party, not a western association." His request was granted, and from that time on the party ceased to observe democratic procedures. Hitler had become the supreme leader, the *Führer,* and he demanded absolute obedience from his followers.

While Adolf was consolidating his grip on the Nazi party, another right-wing leader, Benito Mussolini, was rising to power in Italy. Mussolini commanded the Fascist party, which took its name from the Latin word *fasces*—a bundle of rods bound around an ax handle with the blade protruding at the top. The fasces was a symbol of power in ancient Rome. Mussolini and his troops, known as the Blackshirts because of their black uniforms, had recently occupied Ravenna and other Italian cities. Now they were getting ready to march on Rome.

There were many similarities between Mussolini's brand of Fascism and Hitler's National Socialist philosophy. Both were strongly nationalistic, passionately anti-Communist, and suspicious of the parliamentary form of government that the democracies practiced. Their leaders were similar, too. Mussolini and Hitler both came from lower-middle-class backgrounds, and both had fought in the First World War—although on different sides.

Thinking he could learn from Mussolini's methods, Hitler sent a representative to meet with the Italian leader. Mussolini received the representative cordially, even though he had never heard of Adolf Hitler. The

OPPOSITE: The swastika is much in evidence on the banners for this Nazi street demonstration in the 1920s. Note Hitler leading the salute in the middle of the front row. *The Library of Congress*

Benito Mussolini turns to speak to one of his followers during a Fascist parade in Rome in 1923. *The Library of Congress*

representative asked if Mussolini and his army of Blackshirts would resort to force should the Italian government refuse to meet their demands. Mussolini replied, "We shall *be* the government, because it is our will!"

Hitler was greatly impressed when told of Mussolini's remark, and even more impressed a few weeks later when Mussolini and his Blackshirts entered Rome without a fight on October 28, 1922, and took control of Italy. It proved what could be accomplished by sheer nerve— a lesson that Hitler would take to heart in the months and years to come.

By the end of 1922, Hitler had given speech after speech to ever-more-enthusiastic crowds. One rally in Munich drew more than 50,000 excited, cheering spectators. Many of those who heard Hitler agreed with his vision of a strong Germany and signed on as new members of the National Socialist Party They came from all walks of life—from petty criminals with nothing to lose, to war veterans resentful that Germany had been defeated, to middle-class professionals who had seen their hard-earned savings vanish in the postwar inflation. They were united by their mistrust of the Weimar Republic and their desire for a strong leader who would do whatever he deemed necessary to solve Germany's problems.

Among those drawn to Hitler at this time were three men who would remain his loyal followers in the years to come. One was Rudolf Hess, a shy, bookish person on the surface, who believed that a leader "does not shrink from bloodshed. Great questions are always decided by blood and iron." Another was Julius Streicher, a fanatical anti-Semite, who founded the Nazi Party branch in the city of Nuremberg and then launched *Der Stürmer* (The Storm Trooper), a weekly newspaper dedicated to attacking the Jews.

Perhaps the most influential of Hitler's new supporters was Hermann Göring, a World War One air ace who was looking for a cause and found it in the Nazi Party. Göring later described his reactions to the first speech of Hitler's that he heard. "'You've got to have bayonets to back up your threats,' he said. Well, *that* was what I wanted to hear. He wanted to build up a party that would make Germany strong and smash the Treaty of Versailles. Well, I said to myself, *that's* the party for me!" Hitler appreciated Göring's military abilities and assigned him immediately to help Ernst Röhm organize the *Sturmabteilung* (Storm Detachment). Called the SA for short, the *Sturmabteilung* was a private army that had recently been formed within the Party.

Although Hitler's fame was growing, he continued to live modestly, drawing only a small salary from party funds. His home was still the run-down Munich boarding house, but by this time he had rented a larger, warmer room. Sharing it was the replacement for his beloved Fuchsl, a large dog whom he named Wolf. For human companionship he frequented the cafés and coffeehouses for which Munich was famous. Sitting at a table in a quiet corner, he would try out his latest ideas on his followers.

One of his newest admirers was Ernst Hanfstaengl, a wealthy publisher

Hermann Göring in his SA commander's uniform in 1923. *The Library of Congress*

of art books. Nicknamed Putzi ("cute little fellow"), Hanfstaengl actually stood six feet four. He had an unusual background: His father was an aristocratic German, while his mother came from a prominent New England family. Hanfstaengl's beautiful wife, Helene, was an American of German descent. The couple welcomed Hitler into their home and introduced him to the social circle in which they moved—bankers, industrialists, writers, musicians, and artists.

Hitler was awed by these movers and shakers of German society, the likes of whom he had never met before. They, in turn, were impressed by this magnetic politician, who was drawing such huge crowds to his rallies. In later years, many of them would provide financial backing to Hitler and his National Socialist Party.

When he visited the Hanfstaengl home, Adolf enjoyed playing games with their young son, Egon, who called him Uncle Dolf. Egon's mother, Helene, described the Hitler she observed at that time: "He was a slim, shy young man, with a faraway look in his very blue eyes. He dressed almost shabbily—a cheap white shirt, black tie, a worn blue suit, a beige-colored trench coat, much the worse for wear. . . . His appearance was [really] quite pathetic."

Hitler in 1923, in the worn trench coat that Helene Hanfstaengl described.
The Library of Congress

The Hanfstaengls were curious about his private life, and one day Hitler admitted to them that he really didn't have any. He went on to say that the audiences at his speeches gave him the emotional satisfaction he might otherwise have sought from a woman. He also told them that he would never marry: "My only bride is my Motherland," he stated firmly.

By the fall of 1923, Hitler decided it was time for the Nazi Party to assert itself. Under his leadership, the Party would launch a putsch, a coup, in Munich. Once he and his allies had seized power in the city, they would consolidate their hold on the rest of Bavaria. Then they would march north to Berlin, where they would confront and overthrow the weak national government of Chancellor Gustav Stresemann. If Benito Mussolini could lead his Blackshirts into Rome and take control of Italy, why couldn't he, Adolf Hitler, bring off a similarly bold action in Germany?

Conditions in Bavaria and the country as a whole seemed ripe for such a revolution. The galloping inflation rate meant that the value of money changed not by the week or month, but by the hour. In October 1923, it took more than 6 million marks—the standard currency—to equal one prewar mark. Office managers making a salary of 2 billion marks a week could afford to buy only potatoes to feed their families. In a desperate situation such as this, people looked to a leader like Hitler to point a way out of their misery. As a result, the Nazi Party grew dramatically in 1923; between January and mid-October, 35,000 new members joined its ranks. And much of the Party's membership lived in Bavaria.

At this time, the Bavarian government was dominated by three leaders: the conservative civilian commissioner, Gustav von Kahr; General Otto von Lossow, commander of the army; and Colonel Hans von Seisser, chief of the secret police. They felt menaced by the rising influence of Hitler and his Nazi followers, but refrained from cracking down on the Party because they realized the Nazis had many supporters in the army and the police, and among the Bavarian people. Instead of confronting Hitler directly, the three leaders decided to hold a mass patriotic rally in one of Munich's largest beer halls to explain their own political aims.

Hitler saw the rally as a perfect opportunity to start the uprising. The beer hall was a rambling building, surrounded by gardens and containing a number of dining rooms and bars. The main hall could hold 3,000 people, most of whom would probably be sympathetic to the Nazi cause. With all three civic leaders on the same speakers' platform, it should be a relatively simple matter to interrupt the proceedings, escort the three to a private room, and either convince them to join the takeover or, if need be, imprison them. But Hitler hoped he could gain their cooperation.

At first everything went according to plan. Hitler arrived at the beer hall a little after eight o'clock on the evening of November 8. He stood quietly by a pillar in the crowded hall, sipping a beer and waiting for his SA bodyguards to get there. Meanwhile, trucks filled with other Nazi storm troopers pulled up to the beer hall. The armed troopers jumped out and quickly surrounded the building, stationing guards at all the entrances. Confused and outnumbered, the municipal police on duty did nothing to stop them.

Captain Hermann Göring, the SA bodyguard unit, and Rudolf Hess entered the hall shortly after eight-thirty. Hitler put down his beer, removed his pistol from its holster, and joined Göring and the others. The bodyguards shouted, "Heil Hitler!" ("Hail Hitler!") and brandished their weapons as the group moved through the crowd toward the speakers' platform. When their way was blocked, Hitler climbed onto a chair, waved his pistol in the air, and yelled, "Quiet!" The uproar continued, so he fired a round into the ceiling. Then, in the stunned silence, he said, "The national revolution has broken out! The hall is surrounded!"

The crowd remained silent under the watchful gaze of Göring and the bodyguards as Hitler spoke with the three Bavarian leaders and led them off to a side room. Before he left, he turned to assure the crowd that everything would be settled in ten minutes. In the side room, Hitler tried to win over the three leaders by saying that his only goal was to save Germany from the twin evils of republicanism and Communism, and by promising them important positions in the new national government he planned to form. He stressed that General Ludendorff supported the revolution, hoping this would impress them.

The leaders were still not convinced when shouts from outside alarmed Hitler and made him return to the hall. There he overcame the impatient crowd's boos and jeers with a passionate speech that seemed to convince even his most skeptical listeners. "Outside are Kahr, Lossow, and Seisser," Hitler concluded. "They are struggling hard to reach a decision. May I say that you will stand behind them?"

"Yes! Yes!" the crowd roared.

At that moment General Ludendorff strode into the hall. Hitler hastened to welcome him, then ushered him into the side room where the three Bavarian leaders were still waiting. Within a short time, the general had persuaded the two military leaders to accept Hitler's plan, and eventually Commissioner Kahr gave his assent also. Hitler led the way back to the hall, where the crowd erupted into cheers and loud applause when they heard that an agreement had been reached.

Hitler was triumphant. His voice trembled with emotion as he said, "I am going to fulfill the vow I made to myself five years ago when I was a blind cripple in the military hospital: to know neither rest nor peace until the November criminals have been overthrown, until on the ruins of the wretched Germany of today there shall have arisen once more a Germany of power and greatness, of freedom and splendor!"

Thrilled by his words, the crowd in the hall rose to its feet and started to sing the national anthem, *Deutschland über Alles* ("Germany over All"). A beaming Hitler made his way through the mass of people, shaking hands to the right and left. At that moment, it seemed as if the Nazi revolution was destined for complete success.

7 · ARRESTED

NOT ALL THE EVENTS in the uprising took place in the beer hall. While Hitler and Ludendorff were gaining the consent of Bavaria's leaders, Captain Ernst Röhm was addressing 2,000 SA supporters in another Munich hall. Hitler phoned to inform the crowd there that the Nazi coup had succeeded. He then ordered Röhm to proceed with his men to the army's headquarters in Munich and occupy the building. Röhm did so at once, and seized the premises without a struggle. But he neglected one important thing: He left an officer who was opposed to the revolution in charge of the telephone switchboard.

Back at the beer hall, Hitler received word that a problem had developed at one of the military barracks in the city. He decided to settle the matter personally, and left General Ludendorff in charge of the situation at the hall. This turned out to be a serious mistake, for as soon as Hitler left, General Lossow told Ludendorff he needed to go to his office to issue orders concerning the revolution. The other Bavarian leaders said they had to go, too, and Ludendorff took them at their word. He granted permission for them all to leave, and the three hurried out of the hall.

When Hitler returned to the beer hall and heard that the leaders had left, he was furious. Ludendorff defended his action, saying the men had given their word earlier that they would support the uprising, and he was sure they would keep it. Hitler wasn't so sure, and as the events of the night played out, he was right. General Lossow phoned his military headquarters and told the telephone operator that he and the other Bavarian leaders had managed to escape and were organizing a counterattack against Hitler and his fellow Nazis. The general asked the operator to alert all the military battalions that still supported Lossow and the Bavarian government.

Hitler was now at army headquarters with Röhm, who had finally become suspicious of the telephone operator in the next room. But by the time Röhm ordered the operator's arrest, the man had managed to transmit all of General Lossow's orders. Shortly before three A.M., the general sent out a message to all German wireless stations. It read in part, "State Commissioner v. Kahr, Col. v. Seisser, and General v. Lossow repudiate the Hitler putsch. Expressions of support extracted at gunpoint are invalid."

Safe at the barracks of an infantry regiment, Commissioner Kahr issued a proclamation. "Had the senseless and purposeless attempt at revolt succeeded," it said, "Germany would have been plunged into the abyss and Bavaria with it." He ordered that the Nazi Party and other right-wing organizations be dissolved immediately, and stated that all those responsible for the revolt, especially Adolf Hitler, would "ruthlessly be made to suffer the punishment they deserve."

Word of Kahr's proclamation reached Hitler as he was about to leave the military headquarters, which was still under Captain Röhm's control, and return to the beer hall. He was depressed by the news but vowed to fight on. When morning came, and the ordinary citizens of Munich left their homes for work, it was unclear who was in charge in the city. The Nazi flag with its bold swastika flew over some public buildings, while policemen put up posters denouncing the Nazis on the walls below.

At the beer hall, Hitler, General Ludendorff, and Captain Göring received word that Röhm was besieged at the military headquarters by troops from the army and state police. Hitler decided to organize a march from the beer hall to the headquarters to relieve Röhm and his men. He was convinced that hundreds of onlookers would lend their support to the Nazis and join the march, ensuring its success. "After all," he said, "those gentlemen [Kahr, Lossow, and Seisser] would hardly be foolish enough to use machine guns against a general uprising of the people."

Ludendorff, too, was convinced that army troops would not stop the march. "The Heavens will fall before the Bavarian army turns against me," he said. And so, shortly before noon, 2,000 people set out from the beer hall. In the vanguard were eight men carrying swastika banners. Behind them came the leaders of the Nazi Party, Hitler and Ludendorff.

An SA unit prepares to leave the beer hall for the march to Munich's military head-quarters. *The Library of Congress*

Hitler wore his familiar trench coat and carried a slouch hat; his face was set in a grim expression.

Following the leaders were the elite troops of the Party, Hitler's hundred-man bodyguard, and the smartly trained members of Göring's SA regiment. In the rear marched a motley assortment of Nazi supporters: war veterans dressed in all or part of their old uniforms, college students, laborers in their work clothes, middle-aged businessmen in suits. The SA men were armed with pistols, and some of the others carried rifles or fixed bayonets. But all of those marching had one item of dress in common: a swastika armband worn on the left arm.

As the marchers approached a bridge leading to the heart of the city, a small force of state police moved to stop them. The police gave way, though, when several of the marchers, their bayonets at the ready, shouted, "Don't shoot at your comrades!" The street ahead was lined on both sides with onlookers, many of them waving swastika flags and shouting their support. Some of them stepped down from the curb and joined the parade. Their enthusiasm lifted the spirits of the marchers, who started singing a patriotic song that began, "O Germany, high in honor . . ."

The parade turned into a narrower street, heading toward the military headquarters where Röhm was trapped. Ahead was a troop of green-uniformed state police. Their commander gave the order to drive back the marchers, but the Nazis did not retreat. Instead, they blocked the street, holding off the policemen with pistols and bayonets. Suddenly a shot rang out, and a police sergeant fell to the pavement, dead. It wasn't clear whether the shot came from the police themselves or from the marchers. Whoever was responsible, the police responded by firing into the crowd of marchers, the Nazis returned their fire, and panic spread as everyone involved ducked for cover.

Hitler's personal bodyguard, Ulrich Graf, jumped in front of his leader to protect him and was hit by half a dozen bullets. As Graf fell, he grabbed Hitler and pulled him down with him. A sharp pain shot through Adolf's left shoulder when he landed on the pavement. The loyal Graf was dead, but other Nazis shielded Hitler and helped him into a side street. Meanwhile, General Ludendorff, who still believed no soldier would harm a hero of the First World War, marched forward defiantly. He was arrested by a young lieutenant in the army, who said he was simply carrying out orders.

Hermann Göring lay groaning on the pavement after being shot in the thigh. Friends hoisted him up and carried him to a nearby house. The owner—after stating that he was Jewish—gave Göring first aid anyway and allowed him to stay until his friends could take him safely away. At military headquarters, Ernst Röhm realized there was no point in holding out any longer and surrendered to the troops that surrounded the building. Those Nazis who had remained behind at the beer hall surrendered also. The uprising was over, but the Nazis still had a large measure of support among the citizens of Munich. As the victorious state police led their prisoners away from the beer hall, many in the crowd shouted abuse at them. "Jew defenders!" they cried. "Betrayers of the Fatherland!"

In the meantime, Adolf Hitler, aided by an SA medical corpsman, had found his way to his parked car, a gift of the Party. He ordered the driver to take him back to the beer hall, but every possible route was blocked. At last they turned and drove out of the city toward Salzburg. Hitler's left shoulder was growing more painful by the minute. He thought he might have been shot, but when the corpsman managed to remove Adolf's jacket and shirt, he found that the shoulder was severely dislocated. The corpsman could not set it properly in a moving car, but he bound the arm to Hitler's body with a scarf so that the shoulder would not be jolted further.

At that point, Hitler remembered that they were not far from his friend Putzi Hanfstaengl's country house. He was sure they could get help there. Helene Hanfstaengl, an ardent supporter of Hitler's, welcomed the trio and explained that her husband was still in Munich. Hitler became more and more agitated as he told Helene about the failed putsch. He bemoaned the death of his loyal bodyguard, who had taken the bullets meant for him, and mourned the loss of General Ludendorff, who he thought had died in the fighting also. He went on to denounce what he called the treachery of the three Bavarian leaders and, according to Helene, "swore he would go on fighting for his ideals as long as breath was in him."

After warning Hitler that it would be dangerous to put it off any longer, the medical corpsman succeeded in setting the dislocated shoulder. That night, Hitler tried to sleep but could not because of the intense pain. The next day, the corpsman and the driver went back to Munich, the corpsman to get a doctor to make sure Hitler's shoulder was properly set, and the driver to obtain the loan of another car in which Hitler could escape to Austria.

The corpsman returned with the doctor shortly before noon, and the doctor reassured Hitler that the dislocated shoulder was coming along nicely. But the driver still had not come back with the borrowed car. Nor did he show up the next day, which was Sunday. By then Hitler was fuming; the police knew of his association with the Hanfstaengls, he told Helene. He was sure it would be only a matter of hours, if not sooner, before they traced him to the country house.

He was right. Late that afternoon, Helene Hanfstaengl received a phone call from her mother, who had a villa nearby. The older woman told her daughter that the state police had searched the villa and were now on their way to the Hanfstaengls' house. When Helene informed Adolf, he panicked and said, "Now all is lost—there's no use going on!" He reached for his revolver.

"What do you think you're doing?" Helene said. She grabbed his hand and wrenched the revolver away from him. "How can you give up at the first reverses? Think of all your followers who believe in you, and who will lose all faith if you desert them now!" She spoke calmly, and Adolf quieted down.

One can't help but wonder what would have happened if Helene Hanfstaengl had not been such an ardent supporter of Hitler and his Nazi Party. He might have acted on the impulse to kill himself—and the world would have been spared the agony that lay ahead. Instead, Hitler had regained his composure by the time the state police arrived. He shook hands with the lieutenant in charge and said he was ready to leave.

Young Egon Hanfstaengl didn't understand what was happening. "What are you bad men doing to my uncle Dolf?" he wailed. Hitler was obviously touched. He bent down to pat the boy's cheek, then shook Helene's hand without saying anything. The young police lieutenant reminded him it was time to go. Hitler arranged his trench coat over his injured shoulder, then followed the lieutenant to the waiting police car. After being arraigned at district headquarters and charged with treason, Hitler was taken to the prison at Landsberg, forty miles west of Munich. There he was led to Cell 7 in the fortress section and securely locked in.

Back in Munich, many of his enemies, and some of his friends, thought Hitler's political career had ended with the failure of the putsch. But those Nazis who had survived the fighting and managed to escape arrest were already issuing statements, assuring true believers that the Party was still alive. "The first period of the national revolution is over," one statement read. "Our highly revered Führer, Adolf Hitler, has again bled for the German people. . . . Now the second phase of the revolution begins."

8 · MEIN KAMPF

ADOLF'S CELL IN LANDSBERG PRISON was far larger and more comfortable than many of the furnished rooms in Vienna and Munich that he had called home. But Hitler still fell into a deep depression, and not just because of the constant pain in his dislocated shoulder. He took the failure of the putsch personally, refused to eat, and became alarmingly thin. Only the visits of friends and letters from supporters like Helene Hanfstaengl brought him out of his gloomy state. These people had not lost faith that Hitler was the leader Germany needed, and in a short while he believed it again himself.

The trial of Hitler, General Ludendorff, and eight others for treason began in February 1924. Ludendorff refused to accept any responsibility for the uprising, but Hitler proudly affirmed his role in it. He stated that he was responsible for everything that had happened, then went on to deny that he was in any way a criminal. How could he be treated as one when, as he said, his only mission in life was to become the destroyer of Marxism and lead Germany back to its proper position in the world?

In his final statement to the court, Hitler sounded his most defiant note. "I believe the hour will come when the masses, who today stand on the street with our swastika banner, will unite with those who fired upon them. . . . One day the hour will come when the army will stand at our side, officers and men both."

Once again Hitler appeared to have swayed a crowd, this time the spectators jammed into the courtroom. When the members of the court left the room to decide on the verdict, many observers thought both Ludendorff and Hitler would be found not guilty. They were right about the first, but not the second. Ludendorff, the popular military leader, was set free, but Hitler was sentenced to five years in Landsberg Prison, with six months off for the time he had already spent there. As soon as the verdict was read, he was rushed out to a waiting car to prevent any chance of a demonstration by his supporters.

In the years that followed, General Ludendorff would continue to be a member of the National Socialist Party, but he and Adolf Hitler would never be as close as before the putsch. Hitler, meanwhile, adjusted surprisingly well to life in prison. The daily routine, which included regular exercise in the prison garden, conversations in the common room with his fellow prisoners, and reading in his cell, was actually quite pleasant. And the food was far better than what Adolf had known in the army and when he was living a hand-to-mouth existence in Munich and Vienna.

In prison Hitler had time to think, and to evaluate the mistakes made in the putsch. When a Nazi Party member came to visit him and get fresh instructions, Hitler told him the Party must pursue a new course. Its future, he said, lay not in armed coups but in the ballot box. To gain power, the Nazis must persuade the great mass of voters that their policies were the best ones for Germany.

The Party had gone underground after being banned by the Bavarian authorities, and Hitler did not attempt to bring it out into the open while he was in prison. Instead, he turned inward and began to write the book that he had had in mind for some time. Untitled at first, it included an autobiographical account of his youth, his years in Vienna, the war and the Marxist revolution, and the founding of the Nazi Party. It also devoted many pages to the three subjects Hitler had long been obsessed with: the superiority of the German-speaking people, the dangers of Communism, and the evil of the Jews.

Helping him with the book was Rudolf Hess, who had surrendered to the police after the putsch failed and who was now a fellow inmate at Landsberg Prison. Hess took dictation from Hitler, then typed up his notes on an old typewriter lent to Hitler by the prison warden. Party friends on the outside supplied Hitler and Hess with all the paper, pencils, ink, erasers, and typewriter ribbon that they needed. Sympathetic prison guards allowed them to stay up after lights out to work on the manuscript.

The more Hitler wrote, the more his attitude toward the Jews hardened. "I have come to the realization that I have been far too soft [on the

A musician plays for a relaxed meeting of Hitler and his supporters at Landsberg Prison. Rudolf Hess is second from right. *The Library of Congress*

Jews] up to now. While working on my book, I have finally come to realize that the harshest methods of fighting must be employed in the future if we are to win. I am convinced that this is not only a matter of life and death for our people but for all peoples. The Jew is a world pestilence."

Over the years, many historians and psychologists have sought an explanation for Adolf Hitler's deep-seated hatred of the Jews. Some have thought it stemmed from Hitler's belief that his mother's doctor, a Jew, did not treat her cancer properly. Yet Hitler had had nothing but good words for Dr. Bloch at the time. Others speculate that Hitler was troubled by rumors that his paternal grandfather, who was illegitimate, may have had a Jewish father. But few people thought those rumors had any basis in fact. Perhaps, in the end, there is no rational explanation for Hitler's hatred. The one thing we can be sure of is that it was an essential element in his thinking from 1919 on, and that he gave full voice to it in his book.

In September 1924, the warden of Landsberg Prison made a report on Hitler to the Bavarian Ministry of Justice. It couldn't have been more favorable. Hitler had been "at all times cooperative, modest, and courteous to everyone, particularly to the officials of the institution," the report stated. "There is no doubt that he has become a much more quiet, more mature and thoughtful individual during his imprisonment than he was before, and does not contemplate acting against existing authority."

Many of his friends thought the report would win Hitler an immediate parole, but it wasn't until December 19 that the Bavarian Supreme Court ordered his release from prison. Hitler was jubilant. "When I left Landsberg," he said later, "everyone wept (the warden and the other members of the prison staff)—but not I! We'd won them all to our cause!" Back in Munich, he received a grand welcome home. His dog, Wolf, whom supporters had cared for, greeted him at the top of the stairs, and he found his room filled with flowers and laurel wreaths. The small table was piled high with food and drink.

Early in the new year, Hitler requested a meeting with Bavaria's new leader, Heinrich Held. During it, he pledged his loyalty to Held's regime and promised to abide by the law in his future political activities. Held was impressed. Later, he reportedly said to an associate, "This wild beast [Hitler] is checked. We can afford to loosen the chain." The Held government did so in February 1925. The restrictions on the Nazi Party, which had been in effect since the putsch, were lifted, and ten days later the Party paper was back on newsstands with an editorial by Hitler titled "A New Beginning."

On February 27, Hitler made his first speech since his release from prison in the same Munich beer hall where he had launched the ill-fated putsch. The speech wasn't scheduled to start until eight P.M., but lines started forming outside the hall in midafternoon. By six o'clock, when the doors had to be closed, more than 4,000 people were seated inside and another 1,000 were clamoring to be admitted. Promptly at eight Hitler strode down the aisle and was greeted by cheers and wild applause. In his speech, he reclaimed his role as sole leader of the Nazi Party. "I alone lead the movement, and no one makes conditions for me so long as I personally assume all responsibility. And I unconditionally assume responsibility for everything that happens in the movement."

No one in the crowd challenged Hitler's authority; quite the contrary. When he had finished, even some of those who had questioned his methods in the past surged forward to pledge their allegiance. The Bavarian government was not pleased by Hitler's triumphant return, however. Fearing what his powerful oratory might lead to, it forbade him to speak in public throughout Bavaria. From then on, he would have to limit himself to addressing small groups in private homes and clubs.

Hitler quickly adjusted to this restriction. He went from one closed meeting to another in Munich, recruiting new members for the Party and raising funds. That spring he realized two personal dreams: He acquired a new red Mercedes and rented a country headquarters—a small cottage—in the village of Berchtesgaden in the Bavarian Alps. There he could relax, putting on *Lederhosen* (leather shorts) and going for long hikes in the hills. He also finished work on the first volume of the book he had begun in prison. Titled *Mein Kampf,* it was published in the summer of 1925 and received mixed reviews. Many critics felt it was both pompous and boring. But it sold surprisingly well, drawing fresh attention to Hitler and boosting membership in the Nazi Party.

One of Hitler's visitors in Berchtesgaden that summer was his old friend Putzi Hanfstaengl. He urged Hitler to expand his knowledge and understanding of the world by traveling abroad. He also volunteered to teach Hitler English, a language in which he himself was fluent. Hitler brushed off both suggestions. "What would happen to the movement if I left it to travel?" he said. "And why should I try to learn anyone else's language? I am too old and have no interest and no time."

While Hitler busied himself with building the Party in southern Germany, Gregor Strasser was working to expand the Party's membership in northern Germany, especially in the city of Berlin. Assisting him with the Party's propaganda efforts was a brilliant young writer and editor, Joseph Goebbels. Goebbels had several strikes against him. Barely five feet tall, he had suffered from infantile paralysis as a boy and had been left with a deformed foot. But he had a quick mind and an even quicker wit, and was blessed with a fine speaking voice.

Publicity poster for Hitler's book *Mein Kampf*. *The Library of Congress*

Goebbels fell under Hitler's spell from the time of their first meeting in November 1925. "Great joy! He [Hitler] greets me like an old friend. And looks after me. How I love him!" Goebbels wrote in his diary. His own political views were more radical than Hitler's, but by mid-1926 Goebbels had come around to the more cautious position Hitler had adopted since the putsch. That November, Hitler asked him to be his personal representative in Berlin, and Goebbels accepted the assignment with great enthusiasm. To prove his devotion to Adolf and the cause, he even broke off his relationship with a young woman who was half Jewish.

By the end of 1926, the Party was better organized than it had ever been. The Hitler Youth movement, aimed initially at teenagers, had been launched successfully. The SA, the party's storm troopers, were put under

Hitler's direct control and transformed into a highly disciplined non-military organization. The SA also acquired a new uniform—a brown shirt worn with a brown tie—and after that, they were often called the Brownshirts. No special significance was attached to the color. The Party had simply been able to acquire a large consignment of brown shirts at a good discount.

In December 1926, the second volume of Hitler's *Mein Kampf* appeared. It was subtitled *The National Socialist Movement* and covered the history of the Nazi Party from the time it was founded until the Munich putsch. But Hitler went beyond that subject, arguing for the first time that Germany needed more *Lebensraum,* more living space—in other words, territory. One of the chief goals of National Socialism, he wrote, must be "to secure for the German people the land and soil to which

Joseph Goebbels.
AP Wide World Photos

they are entitled on this earth." A few pages later he was more specific. He said Germany should turn its gaze toward the east—toward the vast territory of Russia, which, he claimed, had fallen under the yoke of the Communists and the Jews.

Few people in Germany or elsewhere took this aggressive goal of Hitler's seriously when his book was first published. After all, the National Socialist Party was only one of many contending organizations on the German political scene. But Hitler took it very seriously, and his belief that Germany needed *Lebensraum* would have a profound impact on the history of Europe, and the world, in the decades to come.

In March 1927, the ban on Hitler's public speaking in Bavaria was lifted. He celebrated by giving one of his most impassioned orations to a huge crowd in Munich's largest meeting hall. As always, Hitler drank more than twenty small bottles of mineral water during the course of the

speech. When his remarks were interrupted by applause, he used the break to cool his hands on a piece of ice that had been placed on a shelf under the rostrum. After the speech was over and he had answered the last of the audience's questions, he hurried backstage to a private bathroom, stripped off his sweaty clothes, and took a long, hot bath.

The Party's membership continued to grow, and by the spring of 1928, Hitler felt confident enough to acquire a country house of his own in the Bavarian Alps. To manage it, he called on his widowed half sister, Angela Raubal, who lived in Vienna. She gladly accepted the invitation and brought along her two daughters, Friedl and Angela Maria.

Hitler was immediately smitten with Angela Maria, a slender, vivacious girl of twenty who was known to her friends as Geli. If she said she wanted to have a picnic by the lake, he would drop everything he was doing and help her pack the basket with food. But not even Geli could

Hitler giving a speech.
The Library of Congress

persuade him to go into the water. No political leader, he said, should ever allow himself to be seen in swimming trunks.

While Hitler was relaxing in the mountains, Joseph Goebbels was working hard to strengthen the Party in Berlin. To bolster Goebbels's efforts, Hitler went to Berlin in November 1928 to speak to the Party faithful at the vast Sportpalast (Sports Palace). Fearing that Communists might try to disrupt the meeting, Hitler brought with him a large number of his personal bodyguards. These were a select group of young men, aged eighteen to twenty, who vowed to protect the Führer with their lives. They called themselves the *Schutzstaffel* (Guard Squadron), or the SS for short.

One of those who heard Hitler speak in Berlin, and was greatly impressed, was Albert Speer, a young professor at the Institute of Technology. Speer, who later would become a member of Hitler's inner circle, was just one of many intellectuals who were drawn to the Party by Hitler's charismatic personality. They joined the ever-increasing ranks of supporters, which now included unemployed workers, solid middle-class citizens who had been hit hard by galloping inflation, and powerful representatives of big business who feared a Communist takeover above all else.

With financial assistance from the latter group, Hitler in 1929 embarked on a policy of political and personal expansion. He bought the Barlow Palace, an elegant three-story building in central Munich, for use as Party headquarters. And he left the single room he had lived in since leaving the army and moved into a nine-room apartment in one of the city's most fashionable districts.

That fall, his niece Geli came to Munich to study medicine and moved into a room in Uncle Alf's new apartment. Hitler often played the strict parent with Geli, making sure she didn't stay out too late at dances and other social events. But when he himself took her to dinner or the theater, friends said that he acted more like an ardent suitor than an uncle.

Geli was not the only young woman to catch Hitler's eye at this time. One afternoon in October 1929, he visited the shop of his friend Heinrich Hoffman, a well-known photographer. Hoffman's assistant, a seventeen-year-old girl named Eva Braun, was standing on a ladder, reaching for files on a high shelf. "At that moment," she later told her sister Gretl, "the boss came in accompanied by a man with a funny mustache,

Eva Braun in 1930, shortly after she met Adolf Hitler. Eva loved movies, so her boss, photographer Heinrich Hoffman, posed her like a film star of the period.
The National Archives

a light-colored overcoat, and a big felt hat in his hand. They both sat down on the other side of the room, opposite me."

Glancing around, Eva realized the stranger was staring at her legs. "That very day I had shortened my skirt, and I felt slightly embarrassed because I wasn't sure I'd gotten the hem even."

When she climbed down from the ladder, Heinrich Hoffman introduced her to the stranger, whom he called "Mr. Wolf." That was a pseudonym Hitler sometimes used when he didn't want to be recognized. Hoffman brought out beer and sausages, and the three of them sat down to eat. Hitler talked of music and a play he had seen, and Eva responded with interest. The daughter of a teacher, she had been educated in a Catholic convent and could hold her own in a conversation.

Unlike Geli, Eva was rather plump, but her blond hair and expressive face made her seem most attractive. As she described the scene to her sister, Hitler paid her many compliments, "devouring me with his eyes the whole time." When she got up to leave, he offered to drive her home in his Mercedes, but Eva refused. "Just think what Papa's reaction would have been!" she told her sister.

Hoffman followed her to the door and whispered, "Haven't you guessed who that gentleman is?" Eva shook her head. "It's Hitler! Adolf Hitler!"

9·A DEATH IN THE FAMILY

THE WORLDWIDE GREAT DEPRESSION that began with the U.S. stock market crash in October 1929 gave Hitler and the Nazi Party a tremendous boost. By the summer of 1930 more than 3 million people in Germany were unemployed, and Chancellor Heinrich Brüning's conservative economic policy was doing nothing to help the situation. Here, Hitler thought, was the issue that could bring the Nazis to power. All the party had to do was reach out to all those who were suffering in one way or another from the depression—and that included virtually the entire population.

National elections for seats in the country's parliament, the Reichstag, were scheduled for September 1930. Hitler campaigned tirelessly throughout Germany, delivering twenty major speeches in the six weeks before the election. Sixteen thousand people came to hear him in Berlin's Sportpalast; between 20,000 and 25,000 crowded into Breslau's biggest arena. In his speeches, Hitler played down his anti-Semitic philosophy and promised that the Party would find a solution to the nation's economic crisis.

When the votes were counted, even Hitler was surprised by the results. Six and a half million Germans had voted for the Nazi Party—eight times as many as in the previous Reichstag election in 1928. Four major political parties and several smaller ones had taken part in the election, and the Nazis received 18.3 percent of the total vote. This translated into 107 Reichstag seats, a huge increase over the 12 seats the Party had obtained in the 1928 election. The Communist Party also made gains, winning 13.1 percent of the total vote. The Social Democratic Party and the Center Party remained the largest in Germany, but both lost seats.

Hitler and enthusiastic supporters gather in a Munich beer hall to celebrate the Nazis' 1930 election victory. *The National Archives*

Hitler had other things to celebrate besides the election results. His book *Mein Kampf* sold unusually well in 1930, bringing him a sizable sum in royalties. And the new Party headquarters, reflecting its growth and importance, opened in Munich in January 1931. Hitler's office on the second floor was a wood-paneled room with floor-to-ceiling windows. In one corner stood a large bust of his hero, Mussolini, and on the wall opposite the Führer's desk was a painting of his old regiment's first attack in Belgium during World War I. But trouble was brewing between the Party's two guard units, the SA and the SS.

In Berlin, the SA bristled under Hitler's command that they abide strictly by the law. In the early days of the Party, SA troops had been accustomed to using any means necessary, including violence, to get their way, and they resented having to take orders from the Party's civilian leaders in Munich. One unit in Berlin refused to act as mere bodyguards at Party meetings and demanded another assignment and better pay. When Goebbels turned down their demands, they revolted and broke into a Party office guarded by their rival, the SS.

Hitler intervened personally to bring the situation under control. He asked Ernst Röhm, one of the SA's first leaders, to reshape the 60,000-man force into a more disciplined organization. Now that the Party had begun to win major election victories, it could not afford to have the SA tarnish its image by engaging in bullyboy street fights with the Communists and Jews.

To reinforce his point, Hitler replaced the head of the rebellious Berlin SA unit with a trusted SS captain. The leader of the SS, Heinrich Himmler, was delighted. "Our Führer knows the value of the SS," he said to a gathering of its officers. "We are his favorite and most valuable organization because we have never let him down." Neat and methodical, Himmler was a born bureaucrat. He worshiped Hitler and would carry out any order the Führer gave him, immediately and without question.

While Hitler was resolving the conflict within the SA, at least for the moment, a problem of a very different sort developed in his private life. He discovered that his niece Geli had become secretly engaged to his chauffeur. Outraged, Hitler forced the couple to break the engagement, and he fired the chauffeur. Hitler's Munich housekeeper believed he had done the right thing. "He was concerned only with her [Geli's] welfare," the housekeeper said later. "Geli was a flighty girl who tried to seduce everybody, including Hitler, and he merely wanted to protect her."

Others weren't so certain of his motives. Some, like the Hanfstaengls, felt that Hitler was overly possessive. Geli herself complained to a relative that her life with Hitler was "very hard," that he insisted she accompany him everywhere and prevented her from meeting any people her own age. Some of Hitler's enemies went so far as to suggest that Hitler was having an affair with his niece, but few of those who knew him believed the rumors. "He loved her," claimed the chauffeur who was dismissed, "but it was a strange affection that did not dare show itself."

Painting of Hitler's niece, Geli Raubal. *The Library of Congress*

In September, Geli became involved with another young man, an artist from Vienna. As soon as Hitler found out, he made her end the relationship. Deeply upset, Geli left Munich without telling Hitler and went to Berchtesgaden to visit her mother. She had no sooner gotten there than Hitler phoned, asking her to return to Munich at once. Geli felt she had to obey him, but when she arrived at the apartment, she discovered he was about to leave on a political trip to northern Germany with the photographer Heinrich Hoffman. The young woman was furious with her uncle Alf; Why had he summoned her back? she asked. Then she ran to her room.

As Hitler drove away, he turned to Hoffman and said, "I don't know why, but I have a most uneasy feeling." Hoffman tried to make light of it, but Hitler didn't laugh.

After Hitler left, Geli roamed about the apartment. The housekeeper saw her read a letter, then angrily tear it up and toss the pieces into a wastebasket. Geli told the housekeeper she didn't want to be disturbed, went into her room again, and locked the door. The housekeeper wasn't surprised—she was used to Geli's displays of temper—but she was curious about the letter. She put the pieces together and saw that it was a note to Hitler from Eva Braun, thanking him for "the wonderful invitation to the theater. It was a memorable evening. . . . I am counting the hours until I may have the joy of another meeting." The note was signed, "Your Eva."

The housekeeper finished her work and went home for the night. When she returned the next morning, she was surprised to find Geli's door still locked. The girl didn't respond to repeated knocks, so two of Hitler's aides were called. They phoned a locksmith, who opened the door. Inside they found Geli lying dead on the floor, a pistol by her side. She had been shot in the heart.

Hitler was already on his way from Nuremberg to Hamburg when word reached him that Geli had killed herself. "Oh, God, how awful!" he cried, and rushed back to Munich immediately. By the time he got to his apartment, Geli's body had been removed. In the days that followed, the left-wing press made much of her death. There were suggestions that Hitler himself had killed her, or had ordered her death, and that the Ministry of Justice had destroyed the evidence.

To escape the furor, Hitler fled with his friend Hoffman to a house in the country. There the Führer paced up and down in his room, hands clasped behind his back, and refused to eat anything for two days. Meanwhile, his lawyer was taking steps to make the newspapers stop their speculations about Hitler's possible role in the scandal.

When the news came that Geli had been buried in Vienna, with Röhm and Himmler present, Hitler made arrangements for a secret trip there to place flowers on her grave. Upon his return, he plunged back into the Party's business. He also resumed his relationship with Eva Braun, which he had apparently kept secret from Geli. But he made one major change in his lifestyle in the wake of his niece's death. Up till then Hitler had never smoked, and rarely sipped a glass of wine, but he had always eaten red meat. Now that changed.

On the postponed trip to Hamburg, his party stopped at an inn overnight and ate breakfast there the next morning. When Hitler was served a slice of ham, he looked at it in horror, then told the waiter to take it back. "It is like eating a corpse," he said to Hermann Göring. And from that day on, without further explanation, Adolf Hitler never ate meat again.

10 · THE PATH TO POWER

GERMANY'S TOP LEADERS could no longer afford to ignore Adolf Hitler and his Nazi Party. The Party's election victories had given it a political clout that had to be taken seriously. Consequently, a meeting was arranged in October 1931 between Hitler and Germany's President, Paul von Hindenburg.

The President had a long record of service in the German army and had been a field marshal during World War I. Although he was now eighty-four, Hindenburg still dominated any gathering with his six-foot-five-inch height and deep, resonant voice. The President was not impressed with Hitler, who seemed ill at ease in his presence. Later, Hindenburg told a colleague that Hitler didn't have the stuff to become Chancellor, the position he coveted. The most he could hope for was to be named head of the postal service.

Hitler did not dwell for long on his unsuccessful meeting with Hindenburg. Instead, he set out to win support for the Party from Germany's leading industrialists. In a talk he gave in Düsseldorf, the center of the German steel industry, he said that millions of unemployed people, made desperate by the depression, were already looking to Communism for their salvation. That was Germany's most pressing problem, he added, and only the Nazi Party could solve it by stemming the Red tide.

He went on to list the Party's basic policies: elimination of the labor unions, which, he said, were hotbeds of Communism; freedom for businessmen to manage their affairs as they saw fit; and a program of public works and rearmament, directed by the nation's business leaders, which would put the unemployed back to work. Hitler's overall message was clear: If the industrialists wanted their enterprises to survive and prosper, Germany needed a strong leader—a dictator, if need be—who would deal ruthlessly with the country's enemies and restore it to its former greatness. His listeners responded with enthusiastic applause and followed it up by making generous contributions to the Party.

In February 1932, Hindenburg announced that he would run for reelection as President. Hitler knew the Nazi Party would have to put up a candidate, and he also knew that he was the most realistic choice. However, he was reluctant to enter the race. Although the title of President sounded impressive, Hitler knew that the person holding it had little real authority. The Chancellor had the most powerful position the German government.

"I see myself as Chancellor and I will be Chancellor," Hitler told Hans Frank, who by then had become his lawyer. "I do not see myself as President and I know I never will be President." The Führer remained undecided for several weeks, but in the end Goebbels persuaded him to run. With 6 million now unemployed, and beggars on every street corner, the future Propaganda Minister argued that the Nazis were bound to make a good showing in the election.

Goebbels devised a campaign for Hitler the likes of which had never been seen in politics before. Airplanes showered Nazi leaflets on towns and villages throughout the country. Fifty thousand propaganda disks were mailed to people known to own record players. Sound movies of speeches by Hitler and Goebbels were projected to large crowds in the public squares of all the major cities. Hitler and Goebbels themselves traveled tirelessly from one end of Germany to the other, making at least one major speech a day and often two or three. By contrast, the Hindenburg campaign was quite disorganized, and he himself made only one public appearance before the election, which was scheduled for March 13.

The aged hero of the Great War held his own on election day, though. When the ballots were counted, Hindenburg led the field by more than 7 million votes. Goebbels was despondent; he had thought Hitler would surely come out on top. Hitler reminded him that even though Hindenburg had won in the popular vote, he had not achieved the necessary majority of over 50 percent. As a result, there would have to be a runoff election, and Hitler was confident he would win it. "The first election is over, the second one begins today!" he said.

Nazi Party poster for the 1932 election campaign. The slogan reads: "Against hunger and despair! Vote Hitler!" *The Library of Congress*

Hitler, with Joseph Goebbels at his side, addresses a Nazi Party rally in Berlin during the 1932 election campaign. *AP Wide World Photos*

Because there was only one week before the runoff, Hitler decided to campaign by air—something few if any politicians had done up till then. Goebbels coined the slogan "Hitler over Germany!" as the Führer flew from one city to another, making three or four speeches a day. Only rarely did he admit to fatigue. In Hamburg he confessed to the local Party leader that he suffered constantly from outbreaks of perspiration, trembling in his arms and legs, and severe stomach cramps. He feared the latter were a symptom of cancer, the disease that had killed his mother. "I must come to power quickly," he told the leader, "in order to solve the gigantic problems in the little time remaining to me. I must, I must!"

Hindenburg won the runoff, getting almost 53 percent of the vote. But

The faces of Hitler and President Hindenburg appear on this National Socialist Party poster for the 1932 parliamentary elections. The slogan is a quotation from Hitler: "The Reich will never be destroyed if you stay united and loyal."

The Library of Congress

Hitler increased his share from 30 percent to 37 percent, while Ernst Thälmann, the Communist candidate, lost ground, getting only about 10 percent. The rest of the votes were divided among the smaller parties. Some foreign journalists, writing that Hindenburg had been reelected, thought this signaled the end of Adolf Hitler's political career. But not Hitler. Having won the support of more than a third of Germany's voters, he felt more confident than ever of his and the Party's future.

Meanwhile, there was dissension among the ruling Social Democrats. President Hindenburg and his advisers had lost faith in the ability of Chancellor Brüning to lift the nation out of its economic slump. Brüning was asked to resign, and Hindenburg named Franz von Papen, a wealthy former diplomat, to replace him. At the same time, the President dissolved the Reichstag and set new parliamentary elections for the end of July 1932. This presented Hitler and Goebbels with the fresh opportunity they'd been seeking.

Once again Hitler campaigned vigorously by air, speaking in fifty-three towns and cities in less than a month. In his speeches, Hitler rarely talked of his anti-Semitic beliefs. Instead, he stressed the need to confront and eliminate the threat of Communism. This led to armed clashes in the streets of Germany's major cities between marching groups of SA men and Communist demonstrators. The ensuing violence resulted in many deaths and injuries, but few voters thought the Nazis were responsible. Most of them believed the Party's propaganda and put the blame on the Communists.

When the election results were announced on July 31, Hitler could claim another victory. The Nazis had increased their share of the vote to 37.4 percent, which meant they would have 230 seats in the Reichstag, more than any other party. Buoyed by this, Hitler decided now was the time to make his move. He contacted General Kurt von Schleicher, one of President Hindenburg's chief advisers, and told him that he wanted to be appointed Chancellor in place of Papen. And that wasn't all. Because of the economic crisis, he demanded passage of a special bill that would give him the power to rule by decree—in other words, to establish a dictatorship.

Schleicher seemed to respond favorably to Hitler's demands, and the Führer left the meeting thinking there was a good chance President Hindenburg would accept them also. But when Schleicher conveyed the

Führer's demands to Hindenburg, the President exploded in anger. How dare Hitler expect to be named Chancellor when he had no experience in governing and could not even control the unruly troops in his own SA? What about the post of Vice Chancellor, then? Schleicher asked. That might be possible, Hindenburg said, since Chancellor Papen would retain all real power.

Hitler rejected this suggestion outright when Schleicher conveyed it to him. The Nazi Party commanded more support than any other party in Germany, Hitler said, and as its leader he deserved to be Chancellor. Any other arrangement was totally unacceptable.

He maintained this unyielding position for the next four months as the German government went through one agonizing change after another. When the newly elected Reichstag met, it voted no confidence in Chancellor Papen. There followed yet another Reichstag election, on November 6—the third in two years. The Nazis, their treasury depleted, did not campaign as vigorously as before, and many voters, weary of the whole election process, stayed away from the polls. As a result, the Nazis lost thirty-four of their Reichstag seats.

Their defeat was of little comfort to Chancellor Papen, however, for he still could not put together a majority coalition in the Reichstag. As a result, Papen tendered his resignation to President Hindenburg, and Germany was left without a Chancellor. Reluctantly, Hindenburg met with Hitler and asked for his help in assembling a coalition government. Hitler refused, saying again that he would not participate in any such government unless he was made Chancellor. The meeting ended with the two men unable to agree on anything.

In the next few weeks, many Germans wrote to President Hindenburg on Hitler's behalf. Thirty-nine leading businessmen, including the heads of such prominent firms as Krupp, Siemens, Mercedes-Benz, and I.G. Farben, signed a letter petitioning Hindenburg to appoint Hitler Chancellor. But the President could not be swayed. He swore to an aide that he would never turn Germany over to "a house painter from Munich." (Someone had told the aged Hindenburg that Hitler was a painter, and he had assumed that meant a house painter.) Instead, the President appointed General Schleicher as Chancellor and asked him to form a new government.

Hindenburg, Papen, Schleicher, and the others in power were not opposed to Hitler because of his anti-Communist or even his anti-Semitic views. They were just as anti-Communist as he was, and most of them also had an unfavorable opinion of the Jews. Nor were they against Hitler because of his aversion to the democratic form of government. Like the majority of Germans, they had lost faith in the frail democracy of the Weimar Republic and longed for a leader who could take firm charge of the country. In fact, General Schleicher had a not-so-secret ambition to establish a military dictatorship in Germany himself. No, what put them off most about Hitler was the fact that he did not come from the old German aristocracy, as they did. In their eyes, he was a mere upstart from Austria—and a common one, at that.

After Schleicher was appointed Chancellor, he too offered Hitler the Vice-Chancellorship. When the Führer refused it yet again, Schleicher tried to go around him by approaching another Nazi leader, Gregor Strasser, and urging him to take the job. By doing so, Schleicher hoped to split the Nazi Party and at the same time build a working majority in the Reichstag.

Hitler found out about the offer, though, and denounced Strasser as a traitor. In response, Strasser declined Schleicher's invitation and resigned his seat in the Reichstag and all his Party posts. But even that wasn't enough to appease Hitler, who was still profoundly depressed. "I have given up all hope," he wrote to his friend Winifred Wagner, daughter-in-law of composer Richard Wagner. "Nothing will ever come of my dreams." Then, in an echo of his mood after the failure of the beer-hall putsch, he added: "As soon as I am sure everything is lost, you know what I'll do. . . . I cannot accept defeat. I will stick to my word and end my life with a bullet."

As things turned out, such a drastic step was not necessary. Chancellor Schleicher soon managed to alienate almost all of Germany's political parties, those on the right as well as those on the left. By the middle of January 1933, President Hindenburg had lost faith in him, too. Schleicher resigned his post, and Hindenburg turned once more to Franz von Papen. But Papen was not interested in trying to deal a second time with an unfriendly Reichstag. In his opinion, there was only one man who could resolve the governmental crisis and bring Germany together again: Adolf Hitler. "Is it my unpleasant duty then to appoint this fellow Hitler as Chancellor?" Hindenburg asked. Papen nodded yes.

Hitler bows to President Hindenburg after being sworn in as Chancellor of Germany. To the left of Hitler are Joseph Goebbels in top hat (partial view) and Hermann Göring. *The National Archives*

And so, on January 30, 1933, Adolf Hitler was sworn in as Germany's Chancellor and what became known as the Third Reich was born. That night, on a few hours' notice, Goebbels organized a grand parade of the Berlin units of the SA and the SS. They marched through the streets of Berlin, thousands strong, each storm trooper carrying a lighted torch. Bands played rousing martial music, and many of the cheering onlookers waved the red-and-black Nazi flag with its bold swastika. Radio stations broadcast moment-by-moment accounts of the parade to listeners all across Germany, and via short-wave radio to listeners abroad.

As the parade passed the Presidential Palace, the marchers shouted their respects to President Hindenburg. But when, a few moments later, they saw Hitler in a window of the Reich Chancellery, they erupted in triumphal cries of "Heil Hitler! Sieg Heil! Sieg Heil!" (Hail, victory!) They were still chanting "Heil Hitler!" as they marched on down the Wilhelmstrasse.

Not everyone cheered the Nazis' torchlight parade. Most foreign observers found it more than a little ominous. The French ambassador to Germany wrote a friend: "The river of fire flowed past our embassy where, with heavy heart and filled with foreboding, I watched its luminous wake." Nor did the Communists, who still made up 10 percent of the German electorate, welcome Hitler's rise to power. They were well aware that Hitler and the Nazis viewed Communism as their mortal enemy, and they feared what would happen when the Führer put his policies into effect. Many of Germany's Jews, who had read *Mein Kampf* and listened to Hitler's speeches, were also fearful of what the Nazi regime would do once it assumed control.

The Nazis, on the other hand, were jubilant. Before Goebbels went to bed that night, he wrote in his diary: "It is almost like a dream . . . a fairy tale. . . . Fourteen years of work have been crowned with victory!"

11·ONE NATION, ONE PARTY, ONE FÜHRER

NOT EVERY ORGANIZATION in Germany bowed down before Hitler. In February 1933, the Communists launched a campaign calling for resistance to the Nazis. "Workers, to the barricades! Forward to victory!" the official Communist newspaper urged. "Put fresh bullets in your guns! Draw the pins of the hand grenades!"

Whether the Communists would actually have revolted against the government is open to question. But their fiery words had a profound effect on a young Dutch revolutionary, Marinus van der Lubbe. Filled with hatred of the capitalist system, van der Lubbe had come to Berlin thinking great social changes were about to occur there. He was disappointed after attending several Communist rallies, though, and decided that only a startling event would inspire the city's workers to revolt. The young Dutchman's favorite form of protest was setting fires. Now he decided to gain attention by putting the torch to one of Berlin's most prominent and symbolic public buildings, the Reichstag, seat of Germany's parliament.

On the evening of February 27, van der Lubbe sneaked past guards outside the Reichstag, scaled the wall to the first-floor balcony, broke a window, and entered the building. Within a few minutes, he had raging fires going in the lobby and the main chamber. Seeing flames shooting out a window, a police sergeant summoned the fire brigade. First Goebbels, then Göring and Hitler, were notified that the Reichstag was on fire. Hitler's immediate reaction was, "It's the Communists!"

The Führer and the other Nazi leaders arrived at the building while firemen were still battling the blaze. As they toured the damaged rooms, many of which were filled with smoke, the chief of the political police

The Reichstag ablaze, February 1933. *The National Archives*

informed Hitler that the arsonist had been found, hiding in a far corner of the building. When asked why he had done it, van der Lubbe replied, "As a protest!"

According to the police chief, the arsonist denied having any connection with the Communist Party and said he had set all the fires in the Reichstag himself. But Hitler would not accept that explanation. His face red with anger and heat, the Führer said, "This is the beginning of a Communist uprising! Well, we'll show them! Anyone who stands in our way will be mown down!" Hitler's voice rose to an almost hysterical pitch as he continued: "The German people have been soft too long. Every Communist official must be shot. All Communist deputies must be hanged this very night. All friends of the Communists must be locked up. And that goes for the Social Democrats as well!"

The Führer's orders were not carried out—at least not immediately. But after leaving the Reichstag, he and Goebbels went to the offices of the Party newspaper. There they worked till dawn preparing the front-page lead story accusing the Communists of a plot to seize power. Meanwhile, Göring refused to approve the official police report, which stated that the Reichstag fire had been the work of one man, Marinus van der Lubbe. Instead, Göring wrote a revised report claiming that van der Lubbe had had the help of several Communist delegates to the Reichstag, and that the fire was the signal for a Communist uprising.

Many foreign observers dismissed the Nazis' explanations. "The assertion that German Communists had any association with the fire is simply a piece of stupidity," wrote the London *News Chronicle*. Some diplomats and journalists even thought the Nazis had set the fire themselves in order to have an excuse to crack down on the Communists.

Most Germans, however, believed what the Party's spokesmen told them. When Hitler asked his cabinet to pass an emergency decree to protect the nation from the Reds, the measure passed without a single dissenting vote. This was surprising, since most of the cabinet members were not members of the Nazi Party and the decree contained several controversial provisions. Chief among these was the suspension of the civil liberties granted by the constitution of the Weimar Republic: free speech, a free press, sanctity of the home, privacy of the mail and of telephone conversations, and freedom to assemble and form organizations. But the cabinet members' fear of Communism obviously outweighed any hesitations they might have had about the loss of these liberties.

The effects of the decree were felt immediately. Squads of SS and SA men joined with the police to enforce its provisions. They raided taverns and other meeting places that Communists were known to frequent and hauled off hundreds of suspects to prisons and interrogation centers. The regular police rounded up more than 3,000 leftists and Social Democrats and put them under protective custody.

The crackdown on the Communists and other leftists gave the Nazis an advantage in the next parliamentary elections, which took place in March 1933. Almost no one objected when the SS and the SA tore Communist posters off billboards and replaced them with Nazi posters. Nor did anyone question the decision of Germany's major industrialists to finance the Nazis' campaign. The Krupp factories pledged 1 million marks (about $300,000), the I.G. Farben enterprises 400,000 marks; and contributions from other industrialists raised the total to more than 3 million marks. With this money, Goebbels set about blanketing Germany with Nazi propaganda. As a result, the Nazis won a majority of the popular vote and Hitler was able to hail the election as a great victory for the Party.

When the new Parliament met, the first thing the Führer asked for was an enabling act that would give him whatever powers he deemed necessary to bring Germany back to a position of strength and prosperity. The Social Democratic members tried to mount a protest, warning that passage of the act would mean the end of democracy in the Reichstag. However, they were quickly drowned out by the Nazis and their supporters. The vote was taken, and Göring gleefully announced the result: 441 members were in favor of giving Hitler the emergency powers he requested, and only 94 were opposed.

Hitler wasted no time in making use of his new powers. He appointed a longtime supporter, Hjalmar Schacht, to head the state bank, the Reichsbank. Under Schacht's direction, the bank made large loans to the government to finance Hitler's ambitious public works program and his plans for the rearmament of Germany. This flow of money enabled Hitler to reward the nation's leading industrialists, who had backed the Nazis' rise to power. It also helped Hitler to fulfill the Nazis' campaign promise to put Germany's unemployed back to work.

The Führer also took the first official steps against Germany's Jews. On April 1, 1933, he initiated a boycott of Jewish businesses, stating, "I believe that I act today in unison with the Almighty Creator's intention: by fighting the Jews, I do battle for the Lord." Many Germans ignored the boycott, and it ended after just three days, but it proved to be a foretaste of stricter measures to come. On April 7, a government decree removed all Jews from civil service posts in Germany, and several weeks later the "Law Against the Overcrowding of German Schools" reduced the number of Jews in the nation's colleges and universities.

Boycott of Jewish businesses, April 1933. The sign on the display window reads: "Germans! Defend yourselves! Do not buy from Jews!"
The National Archives

Hitler defended these anti-Jewish measures in a conversation with two prominent Roman Catholic leaders. He told them that he considered Jews to be "nothing but pernicious enemies of the State and the Church," and therefore he intended to exclude them from academic life and such professions as medicine and the law.

Intellectuals of all sorts, and not just Jews, came under attack. In response to this threat to their intellectual freedom, many prominent writers and scientists left the country, among them the renowned physicist Albert Einstein, the novelist Thomas Mann, and the film director Fritz Lang. But many others, including the composer Richard Strauss and the conductor Wilhelm Furtwängler, pledged their allegiance to Hitler and the Nazi Party and remained at their posts.

Meanwhile, the attacks on those considered disloyal to the regime continued. On the night of May 10, the German Student Association, a Nazi group, organized book burnings of so-called "subversive writings" in cities and towns all across Germany. Local authorities and police assisted in selecting the books to be burned and removing them from public and school libraries. Few voices were raised in protest, and many librarians and teachers attended the bonfires and hurled books into the flames.

In the Opera House Square in Berlin, Propaganda Minister Joseph Goebbels presided over the burning of 20,000 books by Jewish, Marxist, and other "non-German" writers. In his remarks, Goebbels branded the books—which included works by some of the world's greatest poets, novelists, and philosophers—as "intellectual filth." Among those whose words went up in flames was the great early-nineteenth-century German-Jewish poet Heinrich Heine, who had written, "Wherever they burn books, in the end they will also burn people." Heine was referring to the religious persecutions that had occurred in the Middle Ages, but he might have been describing events to come in his native land.

The month of May also saw the start of Hitler's crackdown on Germany's labor unions, which he believed were dominated by Communists. On May 2, the police, with the help of the SA and the SS, seized union offices throughout the country. They arrested union leaders, confiscated their bank accounts, and shut down all labor newspapers. Few rank-and-file union members raised an outcry, however. Instead, most of them joined the newly formed German Labor Front, a Nazi organization

A crowd gives the Nazi salute as books by Jews and other "subversive" writers go up in flames. Berlin, May 1933. *The National Archives*

in which Hitler said their rights as workers would be protected and they would be better off than ever.

Once the labor unions had been removed as a threat, the Nazis turned their attention to agriculture. Germany's established farm organizations were disbanded, and the nation's farmers were compelled to join a new National Socialist organization that carried out the Party's agricultural policies at the local, district, and national levels.

Hitler was now ready to take the crucial step of eliminating all other political parties. Although not officially banned, the Communists had already been cowed into submission. Now, on June 22, the Social Demo-cratic Party was denounced as "hostile to the nation and the state." Its members in the Reichstag were expelled, and many of its leaders were sent to Dachau and other concentration camps. The camps had been estab-lished earlier that year to house dissidents and other political prisoners.

Fearing that their leaders would suffer a similar fate, the two remain-ing political parties, the State Party and the German People's Party, dis-solved themselves voluntarily. Once these parties were out of the way, Hitler proposed that Germany become a one-party state. There was vir-tually no discussion of the proposal in the Reichstag, which passed it without a dissenting vote on July 14. From that day on, the red-and-black Nazi swastika flew side by side with the black-white-and-red flag of the old Reich on public buildings throughout Germany.

By mid-1933, the nation's economy had improved, most Germans had gone back to work, and the streets of Berlin and other cities were free of beggars. The majority of Germans, from wealthy industrialists to middle-class professionals to civil servants in government offices, supported Adolf Hitler and his policies. Only one major force in the country had yet to take a stand on the Nazi regime: the Roman Catholic Church, to which half or more of the German people belonged. Its position would soon become clear, however.

On July 14, a concordat, or agreement, was signed between Germany and the Vatican in Rome. According to its terms, the church and its priests would refrain from involvement in German politics, while Hitler promised that the Nazis would not meddle in the affairs of Germany's parochial schools. Franz von Papen, who negotiated the concordat for Germany, reported that Pope Pius XI had "remarked how pleased he was that the German government now had at its head a man uncompromis-ingly opposed to Communism . . . in all its forms."

At the signing ceremony, the Vatican representative asked God to bless the Reich. The church also ordered its German bishops to swear alle-giance to the National Socialist government. The oath ended with these words: "In the performance of my spiritual office and in my solicitude for the welfare and interest of the German Reich, I will endeavor to avoid all detrimental acts that might endanger it." In other words, the Catholic Church and its bishops in Germany would not speak out against any future actions of the Nazi regime, no matter what they might be.

In September 1933, Marinus van der Lubbe and the four Communists accused of helping him plan the Reichstag fire finally came to trial. Göring played an active role in the prosecution and was dismayed with the judges' verdict. While the judges found van der Lubbe guilty and sentenced him to death, they acquitted all the Communist defendants for lack of evidence. This judgment severely weakened the Nazis' claim that the fire had been a Communist plot. It also revealed that Germany's judicial system had retained a certain amount of independence from the Party.

Göring complained to Hitler about the judges' attitude. "You would have thought *we* were on trial, not the Communists."

Hitler took a longer view of the matter. "My dear Göring," he said, "it is only a question of time. We shall soon have those old fellows talking our language. They are all ripe for retirement anyway, and we will replace them with our own people."

Now that the nation's domestic situation was under control, Hitler shifted his gaze to the outside world and decided to take Germany out of the League of Nations, the forerunner of the United Nations. He, along with many other Germans, had long felt that the League discriminated against Germany because it had lost the world war. Membership in the League, with its peacekeeping policies, also put restrictions on the Nazis' plans for rearming the Reich.

Hitler didn't want the world to think he was acting against the will of the German people, so he announced that he was submitting his decision to a referendum, a national vote. The referendum would take place on November 12. In the weeks before the vote, Hitler campaigned strenuously for his foreign policy. He received enthusiastic support from the Catholic Church and the nation's media. By this time, every Communist and Social Democratic publication had been suppressed, and all the nation's newspapers, radio stations, theaters, museums, music groups, and film companies had come under the control of the Propaganda Ministry, headed by Joseph Goebbels.

When the ballots were counted, it became clear that Hitler and his Nazi Party had received a tremendous vote of confidence. More than 95 percent of those voting approved Germany's withdrawal from the League of Nations. And in the Reichstag elections that had taken place at the same time, 92 percent of the voters, including many German Jews, voted National Socialist, the only party on the ballot.

Hitler had achieved his goal of uniting the state and the Party. His position as the Führer, the great leader, had never been more secure. Even so, he could not afford to let down his guard. Some elements in the military bristled under Nazi control, and their hero, the ailing Hindenburg, continued in the office of President. Closer to home, the uneasy truce between the SA and the SS was threatening to break down. As 1933 came to an end and 1934 began, the forty-four-year-old Adolf Hitler still had much to worry about.

12 · TRIUMPH OF THE WILL

ERNST RÖHM HAD BEEN HITLER'S loyal follower ever since he had first met the future Führer in 1920. As Hitler had gradually risen to power, Röhm and the SA Brownshirts he commanded had supported him all the way. But now, with the Führer firmly in charge of Germany, Röhm was disillusioned. He felt the deals Hitler had made with the nation's big industrialists and the army had betrayed the revolutionary ideals of National Socialism.

Hitler sympathized in many respects with Röhm. But he couldn't permit the rebuilding of the German economy and the rearming of the country to be threatened by a bunch of unruly SA Brownshirts. When Röhm challenged the army by proclaiming that the SA had a key role to play in Germany's defense, Hitler stepped in. He arranged a truce between the two groups, saying the army alone was responsible for defending the nation. Meanwhile, the SA should limit itself to political matters.

Röhm seemed to agree to these conditions, but within a short time he was saying that those who opposed the Brownshirts were "reactionaries and bourgeois conformists." Now Reinhard Heydrich, head of the Security Service, the SD, and Heinrich Himmler, chief of the SS, got into the fray. The two officials saw Röhm as a rival and resented his closeness to Hitler. Playing on the Führer's suspicions and fears, Himmler and Heydrich told him they had convincing proof that Röhm was plotting treason. They accused the SA leader of planning to arm his Brownshirts and set them up as an alternative army.

Hitler refused to believe Heydrich and Himmler at first, but changed his mind after Göring and Goebbels backed their story. The latter two disliked the SA chief and wanted to see him out of the way. Röhm was on

The leader of the SS, Heinrich Himmler (center), heads toward the Reich Chancellery for a meeting with Hitler. To Himmler's right is Hermann Göring, and behind him walks his SS colleague Reinhard Heydrich. *The Library of Congress*

vacation at a spa in south Germany, along with a number of other SA leaders. Convinced now that his old comrade was planning a putsch, Hitler decided to go to the spa in person and confront what he called the "nest of traitors." Arriving at Röhm's hotel early in the morning of June 30, 1934, the Führer strode into his room and said, "Ernst, you are under arrest." Before the groggy Röhm could ask any questions, Hitler stormed out.

Röhm was taken to Stadelheim Prison in Munich, along with the other SA officials who had been staying with him at the spa. Swept along on a wave of emotion, Hitler phoned Göring in Berlin and told him of the arrests. Then he gave the order to round up and shoot everyone in the capital who had been accused of collaborating with Röhm in his treasonous plot. The list included many of those who had opposed the Führer on his rise to power.

Göring wasted no time setting the purge in motion. One police unit surrounded the office of Vice Chancellor Franz von Papen. When Papen's press secretary attempted to block the policemen's way, he was shot and killed on the spot. A second unit showed up at Papen's home, cut the telephone wires, and put the Vice Chancellor under house arrest. Another former Chancellor, General Kurt von Schleicher, suffered a far

Ernst Röhm in his SA uniform.
The Library of Congress

harsher fate. Two SS agents appeared at the general's home, asked to see him, and shot him dead at his desk. His wife, who tried to come to her husband's aid, was killed also.

Agents of the Gestapo, a branch of the SD, appeared with no advance notice at the home of Gregor Strasser, one of the founders of the Nazi Party. The agents seized Strasser while he was eating lunch and locked him up in a cell of the Gestapo prison. There unknown attackers shot at him through the cell window until he was wounded, after which one of the attackers entered the cell and finished off Hitler's former ally.

Meanwhile, back in Munich, Hitler gave orders for six of the captured SA leaders to be shot at once. He spared Röhm—at least for the moment. When a Munich official protested that there was no written authorization for the killings, just a list of names, the Führer went into a rage. "You refuse to carry out an order from me? Are you in sympathy with that criminal scum? I'm going to destroy those boys, roots and all!" The official hastily withdrew his objection, and the executions were carried out immediately.

Upon Hitler's return to Berlin, Göring and Himmler demanded to know why Röhm had not been executed with the others. The SA chief was the ringleader of the treasonous plot, wasn't he? If he were permitted to live, it would make a mockery of the other killings. An exhausted Hitler finally gave in to the arguments of his deputies and signed the order for Röhm's execution. But the Führer added one special provision: If he wished, Röhm could commit suicide rather than face death at the hands of others.

Röhm chose not to accept Hitler's offer and was shot to death in his Munich cell. As he fell to the floor, he let out an anguished cry: *Mein Führer! Mein Führer!"*

Relatively few people in Germany were affected by the purge. Most of them went about the usual activities of a summer weekend, sunning themselves on the shores of lakes and strolling with their families in city parks. And when the official account of the purge was published in the Monday newspapers, the majority of Germans were glad to hear that the powers of the SA had been curbed. They were tired of being bossed around rudely by the young toughs who made up a large part of the SA's ranks.

President Hindenburg was upset by the harassment of Papen, and he did not believe the official explanation that General Schleicher and his wife had been shot while resisting arrest. But the President was too old and ill to translate his doubts into action. Instead, he signed a telegram, prepared by the Nazis, in which he congratulated Hitler for nipping treason in the bud and saving the German nation from serious danger.

On July 13, Hitler offered his version of the purge in a speech to a special meeting of the Reichstag. "I am ready to accept responsibility at the bar of history for the twenty-four hours in which the bitterest decisions of my life were made," he said. The Reichstag members gave Hitler a standing ovation. Then they went on to approve unanimously a bill that legalized the purge and its executions as "emergency defense measures of the state." Not a single dissenting voice was heard.

By the beginning of August 1934, it was evident that President Hindenburg's health was failing fast. Hitler, who had been attending the annual festival of Wagner's operas in Bayreuth, rushed to the dying field marshal's bedside. Hindenburg's son, Oscar, announced that the Führer had arrived and said, "Father, Reich Chancellor Hitler has one or two matters to discuss."

Hindenburg opened his eyes, stared for a moment at Hitler, then shut them again. He remained silent the entire time. The next morning, while Hindenburg lay dying, Hitler's cabinet passed a law that combined the office of Chancellor with that of President. The law was to take effect upon Hindenburg's death, which, as things turned out, occurred just minutes after the signing.

Now Hitler was both Chancellor and President of Germany, as well as Supreme Commander of the nation's armed forces. He summoned the Minister of Defense and the commanders of the armed forces to his study and had them repeat after him the following oath: "I swear before God to give my unconditional obedience to Adolf Hitler, Führer of the Reich and its people, Supreme Commander of the Armed Forces, and I pledge my word as a brave soldier to observe this oath always, even at the risk of my life." None of the military leaders questioned the highly personal wording, and by day's end, every serviceman in Germany had taken the same oath to the Führer.

On August 6, Hitler delivered the main eulogy at President Hindenburg's funeral, praising his predecessor for his military and political accomplishments. Less than two weeks later, in a special election, almost 90 percent of the German people voted their approval of Adolf Hitler as

Hindenburg's successor. By doing so, they not only endorsed the Führer's program and policies but also encouraged his ambition to become the supreme dictator of Germany.

To celebrate his new powers, Hitler decided to stage a grand spectacle at the next Nazi Party congress, or political convention, which was to be held in Nuremberg in September. The Führer invited Albert Speer, the young architect in the Nazi leader's inner circle, to supervise the design of the pageant. On an airfield outside Nuremberg, Speer erected a stone structure 1,300 feet long and 80 feet high with a reviewing stand at the center. Atop the structure Speer placed a giant stone eagle with a wing-spread of 100 feet. (The eagle was a symbol of Germany.) Behind the reviewing stand and encircling the airfield stood thousands of swastika banners that waved in the slightest breeze. They were lit at night by 130 antiaircraft searchlights that reached 25,000 feet into the sky.

Hitler wanted to have a permanent record of the congress and hired actress and director Leni Riefenstahl to make a documentary film of the proceedings. Riefenstahl had won fame with such films as *The Blue Light*

Hitler and director Leni Riefenstahl watch the filming of an episode in *Triumph of the Will*, her documentary record of the Nazi Party congress of 1934. *The National Archives*

and *The White Hell of Pitz Palu,* in which she portrayed brave young women who risked their lives climbing some of the highest mountains in the Alps. Aided by a crew of 120 skilled filmmakers, she brought her sense of drama to the documentary of the Party congress that Hitler himself titled *Triumph of the Will.*

Seen today, *Triumph of the Will* is not only a fascinating work of film art but also a frightening prediction of things to come. From the opening, when Hitler's plane is seen descending through the clouds toward the ancient spires of Nuremberg, to the climactic march of SS troops through the city's narrow streets, their black boots highlighted by rays from the setting sun, the film is both thrilling and terrifying. The viewer watches in disbelief as one smiling mother after another rushes forward through the crowds of onlookers to have the Führer touch and kiss her baby.

Most ominous of all are the extracts from speeches by Rudolf Hess, Julius Streicher, Hans Frank, and other Nazi leaders in which they lay out the Party's long-range goals, as Hitler first outlined them in *Mein Kampf:*

One of the mass rallies at the congress, as seen in *Triumph of the Will.*
The National Archives

the rearmament of Germany, the expansion of its territory, and the suppression of the Jews. It's hard to imagine how any outsiders seeing *Triumph of the Will* in 1935—especially Germany's Jewish population—could have left the theater without feeling severely threatened.

While *Triumph of the Will* was in production, rumors spread throughout Germany and abroad that Hitler and Leni Riefenstahl were having an affair. She denied the rumors then and later, and she was probably telling the truth. Hitler enjoyed being surrounded by movie stars and other beautiful women, but there is no evidence that he had intimate relations with any of them.

That did not prevent Eva Braun from becoming jealous, however. She had continued to see Hitler during his rise to power, but their meetings were infrequent and left Eva feeling lonely. "Is this the enormous love he so often promised me, when he doesn't send me a comforting word in three months?" she wrote in her diary. "Granted that he has his head full these days with political problems, but there must be time for *some* relaxation."

To make Eva feel better, Hitler in the summer of 1935 found an apartment for her and her younger sister, Gretl, in a quiet residential section of Munich. It was a short walk from his own Munich apartment. But the Führer, busy with government business in Berlin, spent little time there. When he was able to arrange a visit, the couple had almost no privacy since the secret police maintained a twenty-four-hour watch on the building.

Eva was right that Hitler had many things on his mind other than romance. With virtually all power in Germany now concentrated in his hands, he set out in 1935 to implement his goals for the economic revival of Germany. He also took the next steps in what he saw as his special mission in life—the systematic repression of the Jews.

13 · "HEIL, MEIN FÜHRER!"

IT WASN'T JUST PARADES and impassioned speeches that aroused the enthusiasm of the German people for Adolf Hitler. By 1935, most Germans were better off economically than they had been five years earlier. Unemployment was down, the value of the mark had stabilized, and most people knew where their next meal was coming from. They might not have as much butter, eggs, and fruit as they would like, but most families had more than enough bread, potatoes, and cabbage—the staples of the German worker's diet. On holidays and other special days, they might be able to enjoy some bratwurst, a favorite German sausage, and a slice of apple strudel.

Prospects for the future looked even brighter. At Hitler's urging, Germany launched a major road-building project, the construction of a network of autobahns, the world's first superhighways. Thousands of workers labored on the autobahns, which would help to unite the various parts of the nation. They would also facilitate the rapid movement of troops and equipment if Germany ever went to war. Once the autobahns were under way, Hitler asked Ferdinand Porsche, manufacturer of the famed racing cars, to design a small automobile priced within reach of the average German family. Called the Volkswagen, or "people's car," the vehicle carried four passengers comfortably and got forty miles to a gallon of gasoline.

Working conditions in the nation's industries improved noticeably. New factories were built with more windows, better washrooms, and cafeterias that served nutritious meals. The nation's health standards improved also. Germany's infant mortality rate dropped sharply, as did the number of new cases of tuberculosis and other infectious diseases

A cloverleaf intersection on the autobahn, the world's first network of super-highways. *The National Archives*

A crowd in a Berlin park gathers around one of the first Volkswagen automobiles to come off the assembly line. *The National Archives*

associated with poverty. Factory and office workers alike were encouraged to take regular vacations, and the government began to subsidize resorts and cruise ships that had formerly been available only to the rich.

As the material conditions of German life improved, the people's cultural life became more limited. Newspapers, magazines, and radio broadcasts were monitored closely by Goebbels's Ministry of Propaganda and followed the Nazi Party line on all matters. Books, too, were censored by the Ministry of Propaganda, and no works by Jewish or Communist writers could be published. Most experimental modern art was denounced as "degenerate" and removed from museum walls, especially if the artists in question were Jewish. In its place, the regime promoted heroic statues of workers and soldiers, and sentimental paintings of farmers harvesting crops and mothers nursing babies.

The Propaganda Ministry supervised every aspect of the film industry and banned the hiring of Jewish actors, writers, and technicians. However, Goebbels realized that the German public would not buy tickets to a steady diet of boring propaganda films, so he adopted a more subtle approach. The production of comedies, musicals, and adaptations of literary classics was encouraged, with only an occasional movie focusing on villainous Communists or evil Jews.

Winning the loyalty of Germany's young people was a major goal of Hitler and the Party. Educators placed a heavy emphasis on indoctrinating the country's children with Nazi ideals and values, starting in the early elementary grades. A typical pledge that third graders recited each day went as follows:

> *Führer, my Führer, bequeathed to me by the Lord,*
> *Protect and preserve me as long as I live!*
> *Thou hast rescued Germany from deepest distress.*
> *I thank thee today for my daily bread.*
> *Abide thou long with me, forsake me not,*
> *Führer, my Führer, my faith and my light!*
> *Hail, my Führer!*

Other organizations besides the public schools helped mold German children into model young Nazis. Foremost among these were several that might be compared in some respects to the Boy Scouts and the Girl Scouts. The *Jungvolk* (Young Folk) prepared German boys of ten to fourteen to become members of the teenage organization, the *Hitlerjugend,* or HJ (Hitler Youth). An equivalent organization, the *Jungmädel* (Young Maidens) enrolled girls of ten who then, at age fourteen, joined the *Bund Deutscher Mädchen,* or BDM (League of German Girls).

The mission of these organizations was to build their members physically through sports like javelin throwing, and to educate them politically. When a boy was inducted into the Hitler Youth, he was given a brown shirt to wear and a dagger upon which the words "Blood and Honor" were engraved. With the dagger, he would be able to defend the Führer and the nation if called upon to do so. He was also encouraged to report to the authorities anyone who deviated from Party policies—even members of his own family.

Squads of Hitler Youth and members of the League of German Girls marched in parades throughout Germany and took part in every Nazi Party congress. It was the dream of many young Germans to be chosen

Hitler Youth members on the march. *The Library of Congress*

The Führer talks with a Hitler Youth troop at Berchtesgaden.
The Library of Congress

to appear in a parade reviewed by the Führer, and to raise their right arms in the stiff Nazi salute to Adolf Hitler himself.

While the majority of Germans, young and old, were probably content with their lot in the mid-1930s, they couldn't help but be aware that they lived in a rigidly controlled society. The regular police and the SS were always on guard, and everyone had heard rumors about people who were arrested for criticizing the Nazi Party or making a joke about Hitler's mustache. Most people simply looked the other way and tried to avoid confrontations with the police. Germany's Jews could not escape notice so easily, however. Their lives, tightly regulated since 1933, became even more difficult in 1935 after the Reichstag passed two new sets of strict anti-Jewish rulings. These rulings were known as the Nuremberg Laws.

In *Mein Kampf,* Hitler had stated that the Aryan race, of whom the Germans were a prime example, represented the highest level of human

Members of the League of German Girls shoot baskets. *The National Archives*

culture and civilization. The Jews, on the other hand, were, in Hitler's view, the source of all evil. Harking back to the Middle Ages, when Germany's Jews were accused of poisoning the nation's wells and spreading deadly diseases, Hitler charged that the Jews in modern Germany threatened to pollute the pure blood of the Aryan majority. He wrote: "With satanic joy in his face, the black-haired Jewish youth lurks in wait for the unsuspecting girl, whom he defiles with his blood, thus stealing her from her people."

When *Mein Kampf* was first published, it was easy to dismiss such statements as the ravings of an ignorant anti-Semite. Scholars knew that there was no such thing as an Aryan race. The Aryans were a group of nomadic tribes that migrated eastward from southern Russia to India about 1500 B.C. They spoke a language that formed the basis of many Indo-European languages, including Sanskrit, Greek, Latin, German, and English. But there were no specific links between the Aryan settlers in India and the ancient ancestors of modern-day Germans.

Once Hitler achieved absolute power, however, no one in Germany publicly challenged the views expressed in *Mein Kampf*. Instead, those views became part of the nation's governing philosophy. Nowhere was this more obvious than in the first Nuremberg Law, the 1935 Law for the Protection of German Blood and Honor. It forbade marriage between Jews and persons of German, or Aryan, blood, and outlawed extramarital relations of any kind between the two groups. It even forbade Jews to employ Aryan maidservants.

The second Nuremberg Law, a related citizenship law enacted at the same time, stripped Jews of their identity as citizens of Germany. Henceforth only those of German blood would be regarded as citizens and receive a "Reich Certificate of Citizenship." The Jews would be treated as mere subjects, and would no longer enjoy the protection of the law and the courts. If the police or the SS wanted to detain them for any reason whatsoever, there would be no one to stop them. Jews could not own land or, of course, vote.

The pressure on the Jews eased briefly in the late summer of 1936, when the Olympic Games were held in Berlin. The foreign press had run a number of negative stories about the Nazis' harsh treatment of the Jews and the Party's other repressive acts. To counteract these stories and make a favorable impression on the thousands of foreign visitors who were expected for the Olympics, Hitler and Goebbels ordered that all anti-Semitic propaganda be halted. Posters featuring caricatures of Jews were removed from public display, and several prominent Jewish athletes were allowed to represent Germany in the Games.

These measures had the desired effect on at least one American visitor, Anne Morrow Lindbergh. She had come to Germany with her husband, Charles, who had won fame for being the first pilot to fly the Atlantic, going nonstop from New York to Paris. Lindbergh was on an official mission to inspect the *Luftwaffe*, Germany's rapidly expanding air force. In her diary, Mrs. Lindbergh described the mood of Berlin the day of their arrival. "The Unter den Linden [one of the city's main thoroughfares] very busy and strung with [swastika] flags. . . . [O]ther flags, posters, wreaths, etc., going up for the Olympic Games give Berlin the impression of a world's fair. . . . Boy Scouts in the streets, black shorts and brown shirts on bicycles, tanned and strong-looking—Hitler Jugend.

"There is no question of the power, unity, and purposefulness of Germany," Mrs. Lindbergh continued. "It is terrific. I have never in my life been so conscious of such a *directed* force. It is thrilling when seen manifested in the energy, pride, and morale of the people—especially the young people."

Mrs. Lindbergh and her husband did not meet Hitler during their visit, but they were entertained lavishly by Göring, who was now head of the Luftwaffe. Göring invited the Lindberghs to be his guests for the opening ceremony of the Games on August 1, 1936. A crowd of 110,000 cheered loudly as Hitler and the other Nazi leaders marched into the stadium and took their places on the reviewing stand. A former marathon winner from Greece, home of the original Olympics, handed the Führer an olive branch as a "symbol of love and peace." A chorus sang a special anthem composed by Richard Strauss and hundreds of doves, the traditional symbol of peace, were released into the sky above the stadium.

Hitler attended many of the athletic contests, watched with great excitement, and was delighted whenever a German contender came in first. But he was highly annoyed, according to Albert Speer, when an African American athlete, Jesse Owens, won four gold medals. Owens equaled the world record in the 100-meter race, broke world records in both the 200-meter race and the broad jump, and triumphed, with his team, in the 400-meter relay race.

Hitler and other officials salute the opening of the 1936 Olympic Games in Berlin.
The Library of Congress

Owens's victories seemed to give the lie to the Führer's theories about Aryan superiority. But Hitler was not about to modify his views. Turning to Speer, who had supervised the design of the Olympic Stadium, the Führer said that blacks like Owens, whose ancestors came from the jungle, were primitive. Thus their physiques were stronger than those of civilized whites. Because of this, Hitler said, they represented unfair competition and should be excluded from participating in future Olympics.

In the main, though, the Führer was well satisfied with the results of the Games. German athletes had walked off with the most gold medals—thirty-three—as well as the most silver and bronze. A two-part documentary film of the proceedings, made by the gifted Leni Riefenstahl, won first prize at several film festivals and is still considered to be one of the finest sports films of all time. Many visitors, like the Lindberghs, left for home with strongly favorable impressions of the new Germany.

Another national leader, enjoying strong support at home and a large measure of respect abroad, might have been tempted to sit back and relax for a time. But not Adolf Hitler. He had not forgotten the other main goal he had laid out in *Mein Kampf*—to expand Germany and provide its population with more land.

14 · ON THE MARCH

HITLER SPELLED OUT HIS LEADERSHIP methods very clearly in the spring of 1937, when he spoke at the dedication of a training school for future Nazi leaders. "You know, I always go to the very brink of boldness, but not beyond," he said. "One has to smell out: What can I get away with, and what can't I?"

Nowhere was this policy more evident than in the moves the Führer had made to rebuild Germany's military strength. While stating publicly that Germany wanted peace, not war, he more than tripled the size of the *Wehrmacht*, the German armed forces. Then, in 1935, he had persuaded the British to sign a pact allowing Germany to enlarge both its surface navy and its submarine fleet. France reacted angrily to news of the pact, and the Soviet Union condemned it as a threat to peace. But the German military buildup continued.

Early in 1936, with a much stronger army behind him, Hitler decided the time was right to march into the Rhineland region of Germany. The Rhineland, which encompassed all German territory west of the Rhine River and a thirty-mile strip on the eastern side, had been made a demilitarized zone as part of the Versailles Treaty. In reoccupying it with German troops, Hitler knew he risked strong countermoves from France and its ally, Great Britain. Fears of what those nations might do gave the Führer stomach cramps and several sleepless nights. But he overcame his anxieties and hesitations, and on March 7, three German infantry battalions entered the Rhineland.

The Germans had orders to withdraw if challenged by French troops, but they met no opposition whatsoever. France did rush reinforcements to the Maginot Line, the string of heavy fortifications it had erected on its

German troops cross a bridge into the Rhineland. *The National Archives*

border with Germany. No French troops crossed into German territory, however. The Council of the League of Nations convened a special meeting in London and denounced Germany for violating the Versailles Treaty. But the world organization took no further action against the aggressor.

Within a week, the Rhineland had been brought under German military control without a single shot being fired. Hitler made a triumphant tour of the region in his private train to the cheers of the populace and the 25,000 troops now stationed there. "Good Lord, am I relieved how smoothly everything went!" the Führer exclaimed to one of his aides on the return trip. To celebrate, he ordered that a recording of one of his favorite operas, Wagner's *Parsifal,* be played.

Hitler had learned several lessons from the reoccupation of the Rhineland. The first was that words of condemnation by the League of Nations had little effect because the organization possessed no real power. The second and more important lesson was that France and England would back off from meeting force with force if they thought the action might lead to another war. The Führer would make startlingly effective use of both lessons in the future. Meanwhile, he spent the remainder of 1936 and the beginning of 1937 consolidating Germany's position in the world and tending to some pressing personal matters.

In late July 1936, Hitler received a letter from Francisco Franco, a Spanish general who was leading an uprising against the democratically

Germany after the reoccupation of the Rhineland.

elected government of Spain. Franco was backed by the conservative elements of Spanish society: the monarchists, who wanted Spain to be ruled once more by a king; big landowners and industrialists, who were opposed to the government's reform policies; the Roman Catholic Church; and the army. In his letter to Hitler, Franco claimed that his republican opponents were really Communists and asked the Führer for Germany's support.

Hitler was reluctant at first to get involved, but Göring persuaded him it was a wise thing to do. To begin with, it would help to halt the further spread of Communism. It would also give Göring a chance to test in actual battle situations the new planes he was building for Germany's air force. There was little risk of a confrontation with France, Great Britain, or the United States, since all three countries had declared their neutrality in what was already being called the Spanish Civil War. Only the Soviet Union was playing a minor role in the conflict by giving limited aid to the government.

The Führer responded to Franco by supplying his forces with a number of fighter planes, bombers, and antiaircraft guns. Mussolini's Italy was also giving aid to the rebels. Soon Franco's pilots, flying their new German and Italian planes, launched a series of devastating air raids on the cities of Madrid and Barcelona. Journalists who covered the raids and experienced their deadly impact realized they had gotten a terrifying preview of what a new world war would be like. Göring and Hitler, on the other hand, were pleased when they saw how effectively the German bombing planes performed.

In the fall of 1936, although the Civil War was far from over, Germany and Italy recognized the Franco regime as the legal government of Spain. They also drew closer to one another. That fall, the German and Italian foreign ministers signed a treaty of cooperation covering a wide range of political and military issues. Mussolini hailed the agreement as an "axis around which can revolve all those European states with a will to collaboration and peace." Journalists and other commentators picked up on the word axis and started to refer to Germany and Italy as "the Axis Powers."

At about the same time, Hitler signed a mutual defense pact with Japan, which was on its way to becoming the strongest military power in Asia. The pact contained a secret clause stating that each country would come to the aid of the other if it were attacked by the Soviet Union.

While savoring his successes on the diplomatic front, Hitler was confronted by a number of personal problems in the last months of 1936. His half-sister, Angela, who ran his summer home in the Alps, did not approve of Hitler's involvement with Eva Braun. Relations between the two women eventually became so strained that Angela resigned from her job as housekeeper. Following Angela's departure, Eva replaced her as hostess of Hitler's mountain retreat, which had been enlarged and was now called the Berghof.

Hitler's close friendship with the Hanfstaengl family also came to an end in 1936. Helene and Putzi Hanfstaengl separated and then divorced, and Putzi became disenchanted with Hitler and the other leading Nazis. He was afraid their policies would lead to war, and he didn't hesitate to express his views. Fearing retaliation, Hanfstaengl decided his only course was to leave Germany with his son, Egon. They fled to Switzerland and eventually made their way to the United States.

As the holiday season approached, Hitler found himself suffering more acutely than ever from ailments that had hounded him since his youth: severe stomach cramps, insomnia, and eczema. He also was troubled by excessive gas, aggravated by his vegetarian diet. To treat his ills, Hitler selected a successful Berlin physician and skin specialist, Dr. Theo Morell.

Not everyone thought highly of Morell; his fingernails were often dirty, and he had been known to wrap a patient's arm with a bandage he had used to wipe a table. But from their first appointment on, Hitler had complete faith in his new doctor. Morell supplemented Hitler's vegetarian diet with large doses of vitamins, gave him injections of glucose for energy, and cleared up his eczema within a month. Hitler was jubilant. "I was so weak, I could hardly work at my desk," the Führer said. "Then came Morell and made me well!"

Hitler had other reasons to feel optimistic at the beginning of 1937. His brand of leadership had won the endorsement of many leading intellectuals. The well-known playwright and essayist George Bernard Shaw gave lectures and wrote magazine articles praising the Führer, and the writer Gertrude Stein said she thought Hitler should be awarded the Nobel Peace Prize.

He and his Nazi Party had inspired the growth of similar Fascist movements throughout the world. In France, the extreme right-wing veterans' organization, the *Croix de Feu* (Cross of Fire), endorsed the Nazis' stand against democracy and the parliamentary form of government. In China, President Chiang Kai-shek, who was battling the Communists led by Mao Zedong, secretly organized an elite group of soldiers known as the Blue Shirts. "Can Fascism save China?" Chiang asked in a speech to a gathering of Blue Shirts. "Yes, Fascism is now what China most needs!"

Groups in Great Britain and the United States allied themselves even more closely with Hitler and the Nazis. In the United States, the German-American Bund (Bund meaning here a group of people organized for political purposes) staged marches and rallies in New York, Milwaukee, Chicago, and other cities with large German populations. Bund members openly wore a Nazi-style uniform of white shirt, black tie and pants, and knee-high black boots. The banners they carried were often decorated with swastikas.

The most important Fascist organization outside Germany and Italy was the British Union of Fascists, founded in 1932 by Sir Oswald Mosley. Modeling themselves on the SS, members of the Union wore black shirts at meetings and demonstrations and were commonly known as the Blackshirts. Throughout the 1930s, their leader, Mosley, made speech after speech denouncing the British government and attacking the Jews. In 1936, Mosley married the beautiful Diana Mitford, a daughter of the British aristocracy, at Joseph Goebbels's house in Berlin. Hitler attended the ceremony and gave the couple a framed picture of himself as a wedding present.

Hitler's policies did encounter opposition from many quarters abroad. Perceptive American journalists like William L. Shirer and Dorothy Thompson warned of the Führer's long-term ambitions, and the Communist parties of Great Britain, France, the United States, and other countries denounced Hitler's moves against Germany's leftists and his support for Franco in Spain. But Hitler ignored or brushed aside his critics as he made plans for even bolder aggressions in the future.

In November 1937, the Führer convened a secret meeting of his Foreign Minister, his top generals and admirals, and Field Marshal Göring. The stated purpose of the meeting was to evaluate the progress Germany was making toward full rearmament. But Hitler soon steered the discussion to another of his favorite topics: the nation's need for more *Lebensraum,* more living space. Germany's problems, he told his stunned audience, could be solved only by means of force, and the use of force

Members of the German-American Bund parade across East 86th Street in New York City. This street was the heart of the Yorkville district, which had a large German-immigrant population. Note swastika flags. *The Library of Congress*

was never without risk. The nation must not let that stop it, however. Instead, it should proceed with its initial objective, which was to secure its southern and eastern flanks by seizing first Austria and then Czechoslovakia.

Some of the military men present did not take Hitler seriously. They believed he was simply trying to get everyone at the meeting to speed up the pace of rearmament. Even Göring thought that much of what Hitler had said about using force was for dramatic effect. They all were mistaken. As events would soon prove, Hitler had meant every word he said.

15 · TRIUMPHANT HOMECOMING

AUSTRIA HAD BEEN HARD HIT by the Great Depression of the 1930s, and rapid-fire succession of chancellors had not helped to stabilize the situation. Nor had an increasingly vocal Nazi Party, which did not bother to conceal its links to Hitler's Germany. The Austrian Nazis had staged a takeover attempt in 1934 and had assassinated the Chancellor, Engelbert Dollfuss. The Party was suppressed at the time, and its leaders arrested, but now in early 1938 the Nazis were on the rise again. They urged closer ties with Germany, and Hitler responded by inviting the current Chancellor, Kurt von Schuschnigg, to a meeting at the Berghof.

Almost as soon as Schuschnigg arrived, the Führer demanded that all Austrian Nazis, including the assassins of Dollfuss, be released from prison, and that leaders sympathetic to Germany be appointed to several key positions in the Austrian government. If his demands weren't met, Hitler implied, he would have no recourse but to invade Austria.

Schuschnigg realized that to give in to Hitler would mean the end of Austrian independence. He tried to bargain with the Führer, but this only made him dig in his heels. Hitler shoved a copy of a draft agreement at Schuschnigg and said, "There is nothing to be discussed about it. You will either sign it as it stands or else. . . . I shall decide during the night what will be done next."

Caught between Hitler's threats from outside Austria and the threat of the Nazi Party from within the country, Chancellor Schuschnigg felt he had no choice but to sign the agreement. It would take effect in three days, and before then Schuschnigg had to win the approval of Austria's President, Wilhelm Miklas. To put additional pressure on President

Miklas, Hitler ordered German army units to engage in maneuvers at the Austrian border, as if preparing for an invasion.

Miklas reluctantly went along with the agreement Schuschnigg had signed. But when Hitler issued fresh demands, both leaders decided they must stand firm against the Führer and not make any further concessions. Instead, a special election would be held in which the Austrian people would have a chance to vote on whether they wanted the country to align itself with Germany or remain a free and independent nation. Before the election, Chancellor Schuschnigg would try to enlist support abroad for Austria's position.

Schuschnigg's diplomatic efforts met with little success. Italy, not wanting to upset its own relationship with Germany, urged Schuschnigg to call off the election. France, on the other hand, was outraged by Hitler's actions and proposed to Britain that the two nations send a joint note of protest to Germany. The British did not see the need for such stern measures. In an editorial, the influential London *Times* said: "Fundamentally, a close understanding between the two German states is the most natural thing possible."

The *Times'* outlook was shared by Britain's new Prime Minister, Neville Chamberlain, who believed the best way to maintain peace in Europe was to keep on good terms with Adolf Hitler. As a result, the British Foreign Minister rejected Schuschnigg's plea for help in Austria's struggle against Germany. "His Majesty's Government cannot assume the responsibility of advising the Chancellor to take any course of action which might expose his country to dangers against which His Majesty's Government is unable to guarantee protection."

Meanwhile, in Germany, Hitler and Göring were putting fresh pressure on the Austrian government to agree to their demands, and the Austrian Nazi Party was staging one demonstration after another in Vienna and other Austrian cities. Isolated and alone, Chancellor Schuschnigg decided his only course was to resign. He spoke over the radio to the Austrian people: "President Miklas asks me to tell [you] that we have yielded to force. Because under no circumstances, not even in this supreme hour, do we intend that German blood shall be spilled, we have instructed our army to retreat without offering any resistance in the event of an invasion and to await further decisions." His voice seemed about to break as he ended with the words, "God save Austria!"

Later that evening, a telegram arrived from Austria's new, pro-German government. Following a suggestion of Göring's, the telegram urgently requested that Germany help restore law and order by sending troops into Austria. Hitler and Göring were elated. This gave them the excuse they needed to annex Austria under the pretext of liberating it. Hitler issued the order for the army to march in the next day with bands playing and regimental flags flying. He would follow them shortly thereafter. "I, myself, as Führer and Chancellor, will be happy to walk on the soil of the country that is my home as a free German citizen," he said.

German soldiers entered Austria promptly at eight A.M. on March 12, 1938, and encountered no resistance. Quite the contrary; in the villages through which they marched, women and children rushed out into the road to pelt the soldiers with flowers. Hitler joined the advancing army that afternoon, riding in an open limousine. His motorcade passed through the town of Braunau, where he had been born almost forty-nine years earlier, but the Führer did not stop. That evening a crowd of 100,000 greeted him in the market square of Linz, the city where he had spent a large part of his youth. When he saluted the cheering throng from the City Hall balcony, observers noticed that tears were streaming down his cheeks.

The next morning, Hitler visited the grave of his parents in a cemetery near Linz. He laid a wreath against the marker and stood alone by the grave for a few moments in silent meditation. Back at his hotel, he ordered the German Ministry of the Interior to draft a law for the unification of Austria and Germany. The document was sent to Austria's new Chancellor, Artur Seyss-Inquart, who accepted it without question. What else could he do? He had been handpicked by the Nazis to replace Chancellor Schuschnigg.

Now Hitler made plans for his triumphal entry into Vienna. But first he telephoned Eva Braun, inviting her to join him in the Austrian capital. Hitler's motorcade set out the next day and reached Vienna in late afternoon. Every building along his route into the city flew the flags of Austria and Germany, and crowds of Hitler's supporters lined the streets. They cheered themselves hoarse when he passed by, standing in the back of his open car, his right arm extended in the Nazi salute.

The Führer's motorcade came to a halt in front of Vienna's grandest hotel, the Imperial. Long red banners decorated with the Nazi swastika

The tombstone of Hitler's parents in a cemetery near Linz, Austria.
The Library of Congress

Hitler enters Vienna in triumph on March 14, 1938. *The National Archives*

hung from the hotel's facade, and a red carpet extended all the way to Hitler's limousine. When he stepped out onto it, shouts of "Heil Hitler!" rose from the waiting crowd. As he acknowledged them, he remembered the last time he had stood outside the Hotel Imperial. Then, as he told an aide, he was an impoverished young artist hoping to get some money for food by shoveling snow away from the hotel's front door—the door he was about to enter now.

Eva Braun was waiting for Hitler and shared in his joy at the enthusiastic reception he was given. However, she stayed in a separate suite of rooms with her mother, who had accompanied her on the trip, and did not appear in public with the Führer. This was not because he was ashamed of Eva, but because he thought a strong leader must always

16 · "PEACE IN OUR TIME"

HITLER HAD GOOD REASONS for wanting to absorb Czechoslovakia into the German Reich. It occupied a strategic position in central Europe, bordering on Germany, Austria, Poland, the Soviet Union, and Hungary. Rich in natural resources, it was also the most industrialized nation in eastern Europe. Moreover, more than 3.5 million people of German descent lived in the region of western Czechoslovakia known as the Sudetenland. These Sudeten Germans bitterly resented their minority status. With active support from the Nazis, they were determined to follow Austria's example and be reunited with the Fatherland.

But certain factors made Hitler hesitate to move against Czechoslovakia. For one thing, the country had a treaty of mutual assistance with France and good relations with both England and the Soviet Union. Hitler feared that the three countries might join forces to oppose any German attempt at a takeover. For another, he worried that Mussolini would not favor a second expansive move by Germany. To allay any suspicions Mussolini might have, Hitler paid a state visit to Italy in May 1938. There he got the Fascist dictator's assent to his Czech policy. Mussolini made it clear that Czechoslovakia was of no interest to him, and implied he would look the other way if the Führer invaded it.

Meanwhile, the Czech government, sensing a threat from Germany, appealed to England, France, and the Soviet Union for help. France continued to issue warnings against German aggression. However, the French were reluctant to act on their own without firm commitments of support from Britain and the Soviet Union. For their part, the Soviets urged England and France to take a strong stand against Germany but did not back up their words with actions.

Hitler visits Italy to win Mussolini's support for his moves against Czechoslovakia.
The Library of Congress

As for Great Britain, Prime Minister Neville Chamberlain summed up his country's position in a letter to his sister: "You only have to look at a map," Chamberlain wrote, "to see that nothing that France or we could do could possibly save Czechoslovakia from being overrun by the Germans if they wanted to do it. . . . I have therefore abandoned any idea of giving guarantees to Czechoslovakia or the French."

The strongest opposition to Hitler's policy of aggression came from a surprising source—dissidents within Germany itself. While the vast majority of Germans believed totally in the Führer, others questioned his motives and even his sanity. Among them were some of Germany's top generals, men who knew Hitler well and feared that his actions would lead to another world war. Working quietly and in secret so as to escape notice by the SS, the dissidents sent emissaries to England and France.

These unofficial ambassadors met with people they knew in the British and French governments and tried to convince them of the seriousness of the situation. But all their pleas were ignored, and some of their British and French listeners went so far as to accuse the German emissaries of treasonable behavior.

A speech of Hitler's brought the crisis to a head. Addressing a rally in Nuremberg, the Führer compared the plight of the Sudeten Germans in Czechoslovakia to that of the Arabs in Palestine. "I am in no way willing that here in the heart of Germany a second Palestine should be permitted to arise," he roared. "The poor Arabs are defenseless and deserted. The Germans in Czechoslovakia are neither defenseless nor deserted, and people everywhere should take notice of that fact."

The Sudeten Germans responded by rising up in protest. The day after Hitler's speech, all their major cities were draped with swastika flags. Thousands of demonstrators streamed into the streets, shouting, "We want self-determination!" The Czech state police moved decisively to halt the protests and opened fire when the crowds refused to disperse. Several Germans were killed, and scores of others wounded, in the melee that followed. Throughout Europe, rumors spread that Hitler was about to issue an ultimatum to the Czechs, or perhaps even invade their country.

As tensions mounted in London, Paris, and other European capitals, Prime Minister Chamberlain sent a telegram to Hitler requesting a face-to-face meeting to discuss the crisis. The Führer responded favorably to the suggestion, and invited Chamberlain to join him the next day at the Berghof, his Alpine retreat in Berchtesgaden. Londoners cheered the Prime Minister as he took off for Germany. But his conversations with Hitler did not go as positively as he had hoped.

When Chamberlain brought up the fear of many in England and elsewhere that Germany was preparing to use force against Czechoslovakia, Hitler became enraged. "Force! Who speaks of force?" he ranted. He went on to accuse the Czechs of being the ones who had used force to suppress the Sudeten Germans. "I shall not put up with this any longer!" he said. "I shall take matters into my own hands!"

Startled, Chamberlain wondered aloud why the Führer had let him come to Berchtesgaden if he was already determined to proceed against Czechoslovakia. Should that be the case, Chamberlain said, he might as well return to England without further ado.

Hitler did not want to break off the talks, so he adopted a calmer tone. If Chamberlain was willing to consider the plight of the Sudeten people, and their desire for self-determination, then the talks could continue. The Prime Minister did not reject the idea of self-determination but said he would have to consult his colleagues in England before discussing the matter further. He suggested that he return to England for those consultations, then set up another meeting with Hitler.

The Führer agreed, and Chamberlain flew back to London, where he was applauded for his attempt at peacekeeping. However, U.S. President Franklin D. Roosevelt was disturbed by accounts he received of Chamberlain's meeting with Hitler. Roosevelt confided to an aide his fears that England and France would settle for "peace at any price," leave the Czechs to their fate, then "wash the blood from their Judas Iscariot hands."

A deal along those lines was actually in the works. In London, Prime Minister Chamberlain met with the French Premier, Édouard Daladier. The two men agreed that in order to appease Hitler, the Czechs should turn over at least some of the contested Sudeten region to Germany. At the same time, the Czechs should receive a guarantee from Germany that no further territorial demands would be made upon them.

The Czech government at first rejected the British-French proposal, saying it had no faith in any German guarantees. But after seeking and failing to find support from the Soviet Union and other countries, the Czechs were forced to submit to the demands of Britain and France. In an announcement of the surrender, the Czechs said: "The President of the Republic and our government had no other choice, for we found ourselves alone."

If Chamberlain had expected Hitler to be pleased with these developments concerning the Sudetenland, he was in for a shock. When the two leaders met for a second time at a German resort hotel on September 22, the Führer rejected the British-French proposal point by point. Chamberlain was stunned; he had been convinced that the plan gave Hitler everything he wanted. But the Führer employed a tactic that he had used successfully before, first in his campaign to become Chancellor of Germany and later in his attempt to gain complete control of Austria. He raised the ante, demanding that the entire Sudeten region be turned over to Germany immediately.

The three-hour discussion ended in a stalemate, but the two leaders did agree to meet again the next day. Beforehand, Chamberlain requested a memorandum outlining Hitler's demands that the British and French could put to the Czechs for their consideration. At the meeting, Hitler handed Chamberlain the memorandum and then explained its most important provision. The Czech army and officials would have to begin withdrawing from the Sudetenland on September 26, and the entire region would be turned over to Germany on September 28.

"But that's an ultimatum!" exclaimed the British Prime Minister. September 26 was only four days away; the Czechs could never meet such a short deadline. As the discussion continued and grew more heated, word reached the gathering that the Czechs were in the process of mobilizing their armed forces. Hitler was grim faced. The mobilization was a clear indication, he said, that the Czechs had no intention of giving up any territory. He warned that the crisis could not be allowed to go on much longer, and quoted an old German saying: "An end, even with terror, is better than terror without end."

If that was the Führer's position, Chamberlain said, there was no point in further negotiations. He would go home to England with a heavy heart, having failed in his attempt to maintain peace in Europe. No, wait, the Führer replied; he would not invade Czechoslovakia while negotiations continued. He was also prepared to make a concession regarding the timetable for withdrawal. The Czechs could have until October 1 to evacuate the Sudetenland.

Although this was a minor change at best, Chamberlain seemed delighted to have gotten any concession at all from Hitler. He promised to transmit the revised memorandum to the Czechs as soon as possible. For his part, the Führer assured Chamberlain that the Sudeten problem was the last territorial demand he would make in Europe. The Prime Minister took him at his word. As he told his cabinet when he returned to England, "I am sure Herr Hitler would not deliberately deceive a man whom he respected and with whom he had been in negotiation."

Not everyone in Chamberlain's cabinet was as trusting. Hitler's new demands deeply troubled many of the cabinet members, including the Foreign Secretary, Edward Wood, Earl of Halifax. "I cannot rid my mind of the fact that Herr Hitler has given us nothing and that he is dictating terms," Lord Halifax said. "It is as though he had won a war without having had to fight."

Czech government leaders were even more upset by the German memorandum and pledged to do everything in their power to resist it. France, too, said it could not stand idly by and watch Hitler seize the Sudetenland. But in conversations with Chamberlain, the French representatives stopped short of saying they would go to war to defend the Czechs.

Unable to win firm support from his allies or his own government, Prime Minister Chamberlain decided to write Hitler a personal letter. In it, he told the Führer that the Czechs had rejected the latest German memorandum and suggested that a joint commission be appointed to implement the changes regarding the Sudetenland that the Czechs had agreed to earlier. Otherwise, Chamberlain concluded, France would probably go to war on the side of the Czechs, and Great Britain would most likely be drawn into the conflict.

When Chamberlain's envoy finished reading the letter aloud to him, Hitler flew into a rage and began pacing up and down the room. The Germans in the Sudetenland were being treated like scum, he said. "On the first of October I shall have Czechoslovakia where I want her!" he shouted. "And if France and England decide to go to war over it, let them!"

That evening the Führer gave an impassioned speech to an overflow crowd in Berlin's Sportpalast. As the crowd cheered, he laid the entire blame for the current crisis on the Czech President, Eduard Beneš. "Beneš now holds the decision in his hand," Hitler said. "Peace or war! Either he will now accept this offer and at last give Germans their freedom, or we will take this freedom for ourselves!" All Germany was united with him, Hitler said, and the crowd in the stadium screamed its agreement. "We are determined! Let Herr Beneš choose!"

Hitler's speech sent shock waves through Europe and America. In London, volunteers dug air raid shelters, and hospitals were evacuated. Thousands of residents of Paris left the capital in search of safe havens in the countryside. President Roosevelt sent two cables to Hitler, urging him to continue negotiating in order to avert the threat of war.

In Germany, meanwhile, the opponents of Hitler—who earlier had tried to alert western governments about his ambitions—were now organizing a plot against him. Its mission: to remove the Nazis from power and prevent another war. Led by dissident generals, the plotters planned a coup. The moment the Führer moved against Czechoslovakia,

"GOOSE-STEPPING, NEVILLE?"

American political cartoon questions Prime Minister Neville Chamberlain's negotiating the fate of Czechoslovakia with Hitler and Mussolini. *The Library of Congress*

their shock troops would enter the Reich Chancellery and other government offices and arrest the top Nazi leaders. When the Führer was located, he would be shot on the spot. The plotters had decided it would be too risky merely to arrest Hitler and put him on trial. He might somehow survive and rise again, as he had after the Munich beer-hall putsch in 1923.

The plotters made detailed plans for the takeover of Germany's press and nationwide radio broadcasting system. Proclamations explaining the overthrow to the German people and the world had already been drafted. They would be issued as soon as Hitler gave the order to invade Czechoslovakia. But that order never came. Instead, the Führer, sensing that the German people were not yet ready for war, sent a letter to Chamberlain indicating he was prepared to resume negotiations.

As soon as they heard of Hitler's change of heart, people throughout the world heaved a collective sigh of relief. The British House of Commons cheered Prime Minister Chamberlain when he told the members of the latest developments. Winston Churchill was one of the few in the House who were not moved. "And what about Czechoslovakia?" he muttered. "Does no one think of asking their opinion?" In Germany, the plotters reluctantly set aside their plans for a coup. It would be six years—and millions of deaths later—before another group of Germans would risk launching a similar plot against the Führer.

Prime Minister Chamberlain flew to Munich on September 29 to meet again with Hitler. This time they were joined by the French Premier, Daladier, and the dictator of Italy, Benito Mussolini. Mussolini proved to be a definite asset in the negotiations, since he was the only one of the leaders who spoke the languages of all three other participants.

The conference began in the early afternoon and continued until the early-morning hours of the next day. The representatives of Czechoslovakia, the reason for the conference, did not take part in the discussions. Their presence had been vetoed by Hitler, who felt it would only complicate matters. Instead, the Czechs spent the long day in their Munich hotel suite, waiting to learn the fate of their country.

At one-thirty A.M. on September 30, the final document of the conference was ready for signature. Hitler was the first to step forward to sign it, only to discover that the ceremonial inkwell was dry. A substitute was quickly found, and the signing proceeded without further delay.

The signers of the Munich agreement. From left to right: the British Prime Minister, Neville Chamberlain; the French Premier, Édouard Daladier; Adolf Hitler; Benito Mussolini; and the Italian Foreign Minister, Count Galeazzo Ciano. (Ciano was also Mussolini's son-in-law.) *The National Archives*

Essentially Hitler got what he wanted: a four-stage Czech withdrawal from the entire Sudetenland beginning on October 1. "Actually the whole thing was a cut-and-dried affair," Göring reported later to an acquaintance. "Neither Chamberlain nor Daladier was the least bit interested in sacrificing or risking anything to save Czechoslovakia. That was clear as day to me."

The Führer, too, seemed well satisfied following the signing. The American reporter William L. Shirer thought he saw "the light of victory in Hitler's eyes as he strutted down the broad steps" of the building where the conference was held. Chamberlain and Daladier were not so fortunate. Before they went to bed that night, they had the painful task of telling the waiting Czechs what was going to happen to their country. Although the English Prime Minister and the French Premier tried to present the agreement in positive terms, one of the Czech representatives could not hold back his tears.

Before returning to England, Chamberlain had a final meeting with Hitler. The Prime Minister had composed a short statement that he hoped the Führer would sign. It expressed the hope and the promise that Germany and England would never go to war against each other again. Chamberlain was delighted when Hitler agreed to sign the document after hearing a German translation of it. The Führer kept one of the signed copies, and Chamberlain took the other home to England. There he waved it to a cheering crowd at London's airport, saying, "I've got it! I've got it!"

Later, Chamberlain addressed another enthusiastic throng in front of his official residence, 10 Downing Street. "I believe we have achieved peace in our time," he said, and the people in the crowd—who only a few days before had been digging air-raid shelters—roared their approval.

There were no cheers in Czechoslovakia, where the new Premier, General Jan Syrovy, made a special broadcast to the Czech people. He told his saddened listeners that he and his government had had no alternative but to accept the Munich agreement, since they had been deserted by their allies and stood alone. "It was a choice," he said, "between a reduction in our territory and the death of the nation."

On Monday, October 3, Prime Minister Chamberlain went before Britain's House of Commons with the agreements that had been worked out in Munich. Most of the members approved them, but Winston Churchill voiced his strong disapproval. He could understand, he said, why the British people had reacted with joy and relief, but added, "They should know that we have sustained a great defeat without a war, the consequences of which will travel far with us. . . . And do not suppose that this is the end. This is only the beginning of the reckoning." Despite the objections of Churchill and other members, the House of Commons as a whole approved Chamberlain's policies by a vote of 366 to 144.

Why did England and France so easily and quickly give in to Hitler and betray their Czech ally? Many reasons were suggested later, including their mistaken belief that they could trust the word of the Führer. They were also afraid of a rearmed Germany—although France alone had far more troops under arms in 1938 than Germany did. In any case, the English and French leaders saw German Fascism as much less of a threat to their way of life than Soviet Communism. If a few small, new countries like Austria and Czechoslovakia had to be sacrificed in order to appease Hitler, so be it. The overriding goal of Britain and France was to avoid a major war in Europe and maintain, as Chamberlain said, "peace in our time."

The only problem was that Hitler had not been appeased. In fact, he was already making plans to annex the rest of Czechoslovakia. And he hadn't forgotten another major goal he had laid out in *Mein Kampf*—the eradication of the Jews.

17 · BEFORE THE STORM

HITLER HAD BEEN LOOKING for an excuse to intensify his campaign against the Jews, and a perfect one presented itself in November 1938. A Jewish college student, Hershel (Hirsch) Grynszpan, walked into the Germany embassy in Paris and shot the first person he met, a minor official named Ernst vom Rath. Grynszpan was reacting to news that his Polish-born parents had been ordered to leave Germany, where they had lived since 1914. "Being a Jew is not a crime!" the maddened Grynszpan shouted to the policemen who arrested him. "I am not a dog. I have a right to live, and the Jewish people have a right to exist on this earth!"

Goebbels played up the incident in the German press, calling it a typical example of Jewish treachery. Thus the stage was set for the anti-Jewish riots that broke out in several German cities when word came on November 9 that Rath had died of his wounds.

Hitler did not react publicly to the riots. However, he made it clear to Goebbels that further demonstrations should not be suppressed if they developed spontaneously. The Propaganda Minister took this as a signal for the Party to organize anti-Jewish protests throughout Germany. But he told the ringleaders to make it seem as if the Party had no role in the proceedings.

On November 10, crowds of Germans roamed the streets, ransacking Jewish shops and setting fires in synagogues. A correspondent for *The New York Times* gave a vivid description of the day's events: "Beginning systematically in the early morning hours in almost every town and city in the country, the wrecking, looting and burning continued all day. Huge but mostly silent crowds looked on and the police confined themselves to regulating traffic and making wholesale arrests of Jews 'for their own protection.'"

So many windows were shattered during the violence that they gave a name to the rampage—*Kristallnacht,* literally Crystal Night but usually called the Night of Broken Glass. Over 700 Jewish stores were wrecked during Kristallnacht, 76 synagogues were destroyed, and 191 others were damaged. Nearly a hundred Jews were killed, and thousands of others were arrested when they tried to defend themselves and their businesses. To compound the insults and injuries heaped upon the Jews, they—not their attackers—were made liable for repairing the damage done during Kristallnacht. And when insurance payments were made to Jews for the losses they had suffered, the Nazis confiscated the money.

People throughout the world were stunned by this latest example of Nazi ruthlessness. President Franklin D. Roosevelt expressed the feelings of millions of Americans when he said, "The news of the past few days from Germany has deeply shocked public opinion in the United States. . . . I myself can scarcely believe that such things could occur in a twentieth-century civilization."

Hitler himself offered differing opinions of Kristallnacht. To a moderate German friend, he pretended to be upset by the violence. "It is terrible," the Führer said. "They [the rioters] have destroyed everything for me like elephants in a china shop." But an aide present when Goebbels reported on the events to Hitler described a very different reaction: "The Führer squealed with delight and slapped his thigh in his enthusiasm."

However he really felt about Kristallnacht, the Führer deeply resented the criticisms made by President Roosevelt and other foreign leaders. If the United States, England, and France were so concerned about the fate of Germany's Jews, why didn't they volunteer to take them in? he asked Göring.

Unfortunately, the Führer had a point. In the late 1930s, Germany was by no means the only nation in which anti-Semitism flourished. The Soviet Union, Poland, and France were just a few of the European countries that enforced anti-Semitic policies, official and unofficial. Despite its democratic ideals, the United States did also. There were quotas on the number of Jewish students who could enroll in many of the most respected American colleges and universities. Jews were frequently denied membership in organizations such as country clubs, and many of the most desirable residential neighborhoods put restrictions on Jewish homebuyers. More important, there were strict limits on the number of Jewish immigrants who could enter the United States.

But Nazi Germany's repressive policies against the Jews were the harshest to be found anywhere. And they would soon become harsher still. In a speech to the Reichstag in January 1939, Hitler spelled out his views on the "Jewish Question" more clearly than he ever had before. The people of England, America, and France, he said, were "continually being stirred up to hatred of Germany and the German people by Jewish and non-Jewish agitators," when it was obvious that all Germany wanted was peace and prosperity.

"In the course of my life I have often been a prophet, and have usually been ridiculed for it," the Führer continued. "Now I will once more be a prophet: If the international Jewish financiers in and outside Europe should succeed in plunging the nations once more into a world war, then the result will not be the Communization of the earth, and thus the victory of Jewry, but the annihilation of the Jewish race in Europe!"

Few people at the time took Hitler seriously when he talked about annihilating Europe's Jews. Even though he had expressed similar ideas in *Mein Kampf,* they still thought his prophecy of genocide was just a matter of words. After all, no one in his right mind could possibly intend to kill millions of human beings just because they were Jewish. Of far more concern to foreign observers were the hints coming out of Germany that Hitler was not content with just the Sudetenland. The rumors suggested that he now had his eye on annexing the rest of Czechoslovakia.

Those rumors proved to be true. In March 1939, Hitler played on unrest in the Slovak part of Czechoslovakia to make fresh demands on the new Czech President, Emil Hacha. Summoning Hacha to Berlin, the Führer threatened an immediate invasion unless Hacha turned over control of all of Czechoslovakia to Nazi Germany. Hacha lacked any firm assurances of support from other countries. Consequently, he felt he had no alternative but to sign the so-called "request" that Germany enter his country to "restore order."

Once again, as in the case of Austria and the Sudetenland, Hitler masked an aggressive act against another country by making it seem like a response to an invitation. This trick had worked in the past, but perhaps

Hitler and Göring lead the victory parade along one of Prague's main streets.
The National Archives

it had been played once too often. Even as the Führer entered Prague in triumph, Britain's Lord Halifax was meeting with the German ambassador to Great Britain. "I can well understand Herr Hitler's taste for bloodless victories," Halifax warned, "but one day he will find himself up against something that will not be bloodless."

Britain did not mobilize its armed forces in the face of Germany's latest aggression. But Prime Minister Chamberlain, under pressure from his government, made it clear in a speech to the nation that Britain would not hesitate to defend itself and its interests if either were challenged in the future. Hitler may not have realized it, but this speech signaled the end of Chamberlain's—and Britain's—policy of appeasement. In the wake of Chamberlain's speech, a fresh wave of anxiety spread throughout Europe in the spring of 1939. If Chamberlain, the promoter of "peace in our time," no longer believed that Hitler could be appeased, where would Germany direct its aggression next? Did the Führer already have a new target in mind?

Actually, he did. It was Poland, the country directly to the east of Germany and the only country that stood between Germany and the Soviet Union. The Führer, as usual, had a good excuse for bearing down on Poland. As part of the Versailles Treaty of 1919, Poland had been granted a strip of land known as the "Polish Corridor." The Corridor cut across German territory, separating East Prussia from the rest of Germany, and gave Poland access to the Baltic Sea. The port of Danzig, located at the top of the Corridor, was made a Free City—a self-governing and independent state—although its population was largely German.

Germans retained the right to cross the Polish Corridor on their way to and from East Prussia, and they had access to their fellow Germans in Danzig. However, there was constant friction between Germany and Poland concerning the Corridor, and the situation had reached a crisis point late in 1938. To resolve it, Hitler's Foreign Minister, Joachim von Ribbentrop, proposed that Poland give Danzig back to Germany and permit the Germans to construct their own corridor linking East Prussia to the rest of the Reich. In return, Poland would be allowed to continue using Danzig as a free port.

The Polish Foreign Minister, Colonel Josef Beck, refused even to consider the German proposal, and Hitler did not press the matter—for the moment. Instead, both countries in the spring of 1939 sought to strengthen their ties with other nations. Fearing a German attack, Poland signed pacts of mutual defense with France and England. When Hitler heard of these agreements, he stomped about his office, pounded his fists on the desk, and heaped curses on the Poles. "I'll cook them a stew they'll choke on!" he was heard to exclaim.

For its part, Germany signed a pact with Italy in which each country pledged to support the other in case of war. While it was being negotiated, Germany celebrated Hitler's fiftieth birthday on April 20, 1939. A military parade in his honor proved to be an impressive demonstration of Germany's military strength as well as a warning to any potential enemy. Units from the army, the navy, the Luftwaffe, and the SS all took part. Examples of the latest German tanks, medium artillery, and anti-aircraft guns thundered past the reviewing stand while squadrons of fighter planes and bombers flew by overhead.

Special services were conducted in every German church "to implore God's blessing upon the Führer and the people." The Bishop of Mainz asked Catholics in his diocese to say a prayer for "the Führer and Chancellor, the inspirer, enlarger and protector of the Reich." Pope Pius XII in Rome sent his personal congratulations to Hitler.

Schoolchildren throughout Germany serenaded the Führer with a song composed especially for his birthday:

> *Adolf Hitler is our savior, our hero,*
> *He is the noblest being in the whole wide world.*
> *For Hitler we live,*
> *For Hitler we die.*
> *Our Hitler is our lord*
> *Who rules a brave new world.*

The Führer basked in all the birthday tributes, and he was buoyed, too, by news that General Francisco Franco had won final victory in the Spanish Civil War. Franco's triumph offered conclusive evidence that the tanks and planes Germany had sent him were superior to those of his foes. This heightened Hitler's confidence as he made plans for Germany's next military move. In a secret directive to his generals, he said the problem of the Polish Corridor had become intolerable. "Since all political possibilities of a peaceful settlement have been exhausted, I have decided upon a solution by force." Preparations should be made, he said, for an all-out attack on Poland on September 1.

In formulating this plan, Hitler discounted the mutual defense agreements that France and Great Britain had just signed with Poland. He assumed that both the French and the British would ignore these pacts, as they'd ignored their agreements with Czechoslovakia, once they were confronted with Germany's unyielding determination. Meanwhile, he decided to launch a diplomatic offensive in another direction. He would try to work out a nonaggression pact with his old enemy, the Soviet Union.

This did not mean that Hitler had changed his mind about the evils of Communism that he had spelled out so vividly in *Mein Kampf*. In fact, one of his long-range goals in seizing Poland was to use it as a jumping-off point for a future attack on the Soviet Union. In the meantime, though, he did not want the Soviet Premier, Joseph Stalin, to put any obstacles in the way of his Polish ambitions. And so he ordered his Foreign Minister, Ribbentrop, to sound out his Soviet counterpart, Vyacheslav M. Molotov, about the possibilities of a nonaggression pact.

Stalin had no illusions about Hitler, either. He was well aware of the Führer's hatred of Communism and trusted Nazi Germany no more than he trusted those other foes of Communism, Great Britain and France. But the Soviet armed forces had been weakened earlier in the 1930s by Stalin's purges of high-ranking officers he believed to be disloyal. The Soviet dictator needed time to rebuild the army's ranks, and a non-aggression pact with Germany would buy him that time.

Negotiations concerning the pact were carried on in secret throughout the unusually warm summer of 1939. German and Soviet representatives argued over the terms while ordinary citizens sought relief from the heat and rumors of war by flocking to beaches and vacation spots. Thus it came as a major surprise when, shortly after midnight on August 23, Ribbentrop and Molotov signed the nonaggression pact in Moscow with Stalin looking on. The Soviet leader even proposed a toast following the signing. "I know how much the German nation loves its Führer," he said. "I should therefore like to drink to his health."

Stalin had reason to be pleased. Secret provisions of the pact, which were not made public until much later, defined the Soviet and German spheres of influence in eastern Europe. Finland and the small Baltic countries of Estonia and Latvia would be in the Soviet sphere, and the territory of Poland would be divided between Germany and the Soviet Union. Germany would regain the Polish Corridor and the third Baltic country, Lithuania, and would control the lion's share of Poland.

When Hitler, at his Berchtesgaden retreat, received word that the treaty had been signed, he jumped up from the dinner table and shouted, "We've won!" After dinner, the Führer led his guests out onto a terrace to view the northern lights. The lights cast a fiery red glow on a neighboring mountain, and the Führer, thinking of his Polish invasion plans, said to one of his aides: "Looks like a great deal of blood." Then, in a lower voice, as if to himself, he added: "This time we won't bring it off without violence."

He was right. In the days that followed the announcement of the Nazi-Soviet Nonaggression Pact, Great Britain and France tried ever more

WONDER HOW LONG THE HONEYMOON WILL LAST?

An American political cartoonist, Clifford Berryman, comments on the unlikely union of Hitler and Joseph Stalin. *The Library of Congress*

frantically to get Hitler to enter into negotiations with Poland. They warned him that they would honor their treaty obligations to the Poles if a conflict broke out. But the Führer still did not take the warnings seriously. Instead, he massed troops all along the Polish border in preparation for a *Blitzkrieg* (lightning war) attack.

To provide an excuse for the attack and win support for it from the German people, the SS staged a series of border incidents on the night of August 31. Disguised as Poles, SS commandos attacked a German forestry station, set fire to a customs building, and seized a radio station from which they broadcast anti-German slogans. Then, at four forty-five in the morning on September 1, German artillery units fired volley after

German troops gather on the border, awaiting the Führer's order to invade Poland.
The Library of Congress

volley across the border. The blasts were closely followed by waves of troops and tanks. The invasion of Poland had begun.

Up to the last moment, the British and French had hoped that Hitler would refrain from taking this fatal step. Even after the invasion started, they tried through diplomacy to get him to pull back his troops. But nothing swayed the Führer as the German Blitzkrieg advanced steadily into Poland. At last, on Sunday, September 3, the British, acting on their own, delivered an ultimatum to Germany. If the Führer didn't order the withdrawal of German forces from Poland by eleven o'clock that morning (noon Berlin time), the British government would be forced to declare war.

Still convinced that the British were bluffing, Hitler refused to heed the ultimatum. But the British weren't bluffing this time. At noon in Berlin, loudspeakers in the main streets informed shocked Sunday strollers that England had declared war on Germany.

It was just after eleven A.M. in London when Prime Minister Chamberlain made a special broadcast to the British people. After saying that the British government had done everything possible to maintain the peace, he announced that Great Britain and Germany were at war. "Now may God bless you all," he added, "and may He defend the right." Shortly thereafter, France, too, honored its obligations to Poland and declared war on Germany.

Hitler did not make a speech to the German people that day. But before leaving for a visit to the Polish front, he sent a telegram to his ally Mussolini. He was aware, Hitler wrote, that this war would be "a struggle of life and death." But he had chosen to wage it, he said, after "careful deliberation," and his faith in ultimate victory remained "as firm as a rock."

Thus began a war that had been brought on by mutual misjudgment—a war that none of the parties involved really wanted, no matter what Hitler said. Until then, starting with his gradual rise to power in Germany and continuing with the expansionist moves into the Rhineland, Austria, and Czechoslovakia, the Führer had always managed to remain in control of the situation. But now he had started down the dark, uncertain road of war and had no way of controlling where it would take him and his country.

18 · ONE CONQUEST AFTER ANOTHER

FROM THE WINDOWS of his special train, Hitler witnessed firsthand the incredible success of the Nazi Blitzkrieg in Poland. On the ground, 1.5 million German soldiers, backed by tanks and heavy artillery, overwhelmed the Polish army, which was composed mainly of cavalrymen on horseback. Meanwhile, fleets of German bombers and fighter planes quickly seized control of the skies over Poland. Within a few days, the Luftwaffe had totally destroyed the small Polish air force.

Although Britain and France had both declared war on Germany, neither of them was in a position to aid Poland militarily. There was no way for French or British infantry to get to Poland in time to join in the fighting. Nor could propeller-driven British and French aircraft easily reach the battle zone. Besides, Britain and France were reluctant to launch air raids on the Germans, since Allied diplomats still hoped that all-out war could be averted.

Meanwhile, in Poland, Hitler set out from his train each morning to rally the German troops. On clear days he rode in an open car so he could be seen and recognized while his aides tossed packs of cigarettes to the soldiers. He inspected kitchens and mess halls to make sure basic standards for the soldiers' meals were being met. "Frontline troops must be assured that their leader shares their privations," he said. But when the first trainload of German wounded arrived from the front, the Führer refused to meet with the injured. Then, as later, he enjoyed being in the thick of the action but could not face the suffering of the war's victims.

By September 7, most of Poland's thirty-five army divisions had been driven back or surrounded. As agreed upon in the Nazi-Soviet Nonaggression Pact, Russian soldiers invaded Poland from the east on September 17.

Warsaw, the capital of Poland, after the Germans bombed it into submission.
The Library of Congress

Caught between two armies, the outnumbered Poles continued to fight valiantly but had no chance of prevailing. Their capital, Warsaw, was bombed relentlessly while the state radio broadcast appeals for "the quickest aid" from England and France. No aid arrived, however, and on September 27, the exhausted Poles surrendered Warsaw to the Germans. Hitler had predicted the war would be over in three weeks, and he was off by only a few days.

As soon as Poland was subdued, the Führer authorized a number of drastic changes in the German-occupied territories. The SS, under the leadership of Heinrich Himmler and Reinhard Heydrich, rounded up and executed all the country's political leaders as well as many writers, clergymen, college professors, and members of the nobility. Hitler looked down on the Poles because most of them were Slavs, one of the "races" that he considered inferior. Acting on his prejudice, he decreed that all Polish colleges and universities were to be abolished. From now on, Polish children would receive only a minimum education, and Polish farmers and factory workers would exist only to serve their German masters.

Thousands of Poles in the western part of the country were forced to give up their homes and farms to make way for German settlers. This was part of Hitler's longstanding policy designed to provide the German people with more *Lebensraum*—living space. Many of the displaced Poles, wandering in search of new homes, died of cold and exposure in the harsh winter that followed.

No group suffered more from the defeat of Poland, however, than the Jews. Special-duty groups of the SS and its secret-police arm, the SA, moved all of Poland's large Jewish population into a few large cities such as Warsaw and Krakow. There they were crowded into ghettos, where two or three families had to share one small apartment. All Jews were required to wear on their clothing a special identification mark, a six-pointed yellow star, and they received smaller food rations than their gentile neighbors.

Jewish residents of Warsaw try to climb aboard a streetcar in the ghetto. Note the six-pointed star on the top of the car.
The Library of Congress

The ghettos became even more crowded when, on orders from Himmler and Heydrich, thousands of Jews from Germany were transported to Poland on freight trains. According to Heydrich, the Jews were to be concentrated in as few places as possible "so as to facilitate subsequent measures." He didn't spell out what those measures might be. In the meantime, new concentration camps were already under construction in occupied Poland, where their existence could be kept secret from as many people as possible. Some of the camps had names that would forever be associated with the extremes of cruelty and inhumanity— Treblinka, Maidanek, and especially Auschwitz.

Hitler's name doesn't appear on any of the documents concerning these actions against the Jews. It's assumed, though, that he was behind all of them, since they closely reflected the ideas he had first expressed in the pages of *Mein Kampf*.

While the orders were being carried out, the Führer turned his attention to the west. He continued to extend peace feelers to Great Britain and France through intermediaries from neutral countries like Sweden. At the same time, he told his generals to prepare for land and air attacks on the west in November before the armies of France and Britain could be fully mobilized. The generals did not protest the Führer's decision, but privately they felt the German army wasn't prepared for a major war, either.

Meanwhile, in England and France, the mood of the people changed from tremendous anxiety in September, when war was declared, to skepticism as the weeks went by and nothing further happened. Members of the British Parliament yawned openly when Prime Minister Chamberlain reported on the lack of any new developments, and British journalists started calling the conflict a *Sitzkrieg* (sitting war), or "Phony War," in which everyone just sat around twiddling their thumbs.

It remained a "Phony War" through the winter of 1939–40, as thick clouds over France and the Low Countries (Belgium, Holland, and Luxembourg) prevented Göring's Luftwaffe from launching air attacks. Hitler bristled impatiently, but there was nothing he or anyone else could do to change the weather patterns. His invasion plans had to be set aside until spring, and when they were revived, the German Wehrmacht did not move west after all. Instead, it headed north in April 1940, conquering the small nation of Denmark without a fight and then crossing the

North Sea to invade Norway. Control of these two countries would enable Germany to protect its northern flank from an attack by sea.

The British sent a fleet of destroyers and more than 20,000 troops to help the Norwegians stave off the German invasion. Hitler became extremely agitated when he heard of the British actions. He didn't see how German forces could possibly hold the vital port of Narvik, but his generals urged him not to give up. In the next few days, the Luftwaffe organized a nonstop series of bombing raids on the Norwegian defenders and their British allies. The raids were so effective that on April 28, the British ordered the evacuation of most of their troops, and Norway soon surrendered. Hitler was overjoyed. Forgetting that he had predicted defeat, he now took credit for the victory. "Why did we succeed?" he asked his aides. "Because there was a man like me, who just did not know the word 'impossible.'"

With Denmark and Norway in German hands, Hitler and his generals once again focused their attention on the west. Two million soldiers, organized in 136 divisions, were massed on Germany's border with Belgium and Holland, awaiting the order to march. Hitler himself worked out the plan of attack. To avoid the heavy French fortifications of the Maginot Line, the Führer envisioned a double-barreled invasion. One segment of the army would thrust through the Ardennes Mountains and drive on across Belgium to the English Channel. Another segment would invade and subdue Holland, then swing south to link up with the first segment in Belgium.

The attack was scheduled to begin at dawn on May 10, 1940. In the early-morning hours of the tenth, Hitler took a special train to his new frontline headquarters, the Rocky Nest. It was located in a bunker carved out of a wooded mountainside on Germany's border with Belgium. There the Führer received progress reports on the invasion and watched as more than 2,500 German warplanes flew westward to bomb targets in Belgium and Holland. He hugged himself for joy when word came that a key Belgian fort had fallen.

Western intelligence agents and Germans opposed to Hitler had warned top officials in London and Paris that an attack was imminent. Unfortunately, their warnings were not heeded, and as a result, England and France were caught by surprise. In the aftermath, Prime Minister Chamberlain was persuaded to resign, and Winston Churchill—long an ardent foe of Hitler and the Nazis—was named to succeed him. Churchill's appointment cheered the British people, but it had no immediate effect on the course of the war. By the end of May, both Holland and Belgium had surrendered, and three French army divisions, along with all the British forces that had come to their aid, were trapped by the Germans in a small pocket of land surrounding the French port of Dunkirk.

There followed one of the great mysteries of the war. The German army was poised for a final assault on the British and French troops, but Hitler ordered them to hold back. Göring, wanting credit for the victory, had persuaded the Führer to let his Luftwaffe finish the job by bombing the Allied forces into submission on the beaches. What neither Hitler nor Göring realized was that the British had organized a makeshift flotilla of more than 900 vessels, ranging in size from tugboats to warships, and sent them across the English Channel to rescue the beleaguered British troops. The weather cooperated with the British, shrouding Dunkirk in fog and blanketing the Luftwaffe's airfields with low clouds. Before the German planes could fly again, almost 340,000 British soldiers had been ferried safely back to England.

Both Göring and the German generals were frustrated that a seemingly easy victory had eluded their grasp. But Hitler was strangely unconcerned, which mystified those around him. Why had he let such a large British force escape to fight again in some future battle? He himself offered contradictory reasons. To an aide, he said, "It is always good to let a broken army return home to show the civilian population what a beating they have had."

Remarks the Führer made to a friend may have been closer to the truth. They reflected his longstanding belief that the British, like the Germans, were Aryans, and thus deserving of greater respect than, say, the Slavs. "Our two peoples [the Germans and the British] belong together, racially and traditionally," Hitler said. "This is and always has been my aim, even if our generals can't grasp it."

In any case, Hitler and his generals did not brood for long about the British exodus from Dunkirk. Instead, they turned their full attention to France, which had been greatly demoralized by the German victories in Holland and Belgium. The Führer moved to a new frontline headquarters, the Wolf's Gorge, on the Belgian border with France. From there he watched closely as 143 German army divisions confronted what was left

Weary British soldiers prepare to evacuate the French port of Dunkirk.
The National Archives

of the French army—a mere 65 divisions, with few tanks and almost no warplanes to back up the ground forces.

Mussolini's Italy chose this moment to declare war on a weakened France and invade the country from the south. Hitler was not impressed. "First they [the Italians] were too cowardly to enter the war," he told Göring. "Now they are in a hurry so that they can share in the spoils."

Meanwhile, the German army moved steadily forward on a 400-mile front in northern France. On June 5, the Germans broke through to the River Seine. Hundreds of French families took to the roads in wagons, cars, and trucks in a vain attempt to flee the advancing Germans. The French declared Paris an "open city" on June 12, meaning that they would not try to defend it militarily. Two days later, the German army entered Paris, marching in formation down almost empty avenues. Only one sidewalk café was open on the grand Champs Élysées, one of the city's main thoroughfares.

Two days later word reached Hitler at Wolf's Gorge that the French wanted an armistice. The Führer could not restrain his excitement. He slapped his thigh and jerked up a knee in an expression of pure exuberance. One of his generals exclaimed, "Mein Führer, you are the greatest field commander of all time!"

In November 1918, at the end of the First World War, the German representatives had surrendered to the victorious French in a railroad dining car parked on a siding in the forest near Compiègne. Now Hitler demanded that the dining car be brought out of a museum where it was on display and placed in the exact spot where it had stood in 1918. There, in a complete reversal of positions, the victorious Germans would accept the surrender of the defeated French.

When Hitler arrived at the site, he passed a granite slab that commemorated the earlier surrender. It was inscribed with the following words: "Here on the eleventh of November, 1918, succumbed the criminal pride of the German Empire—vanquished by the free people which it tried to enslave." Feet planted wide apart, Hitler read the inscription, then gave an order for the slab to be destroyed.

The signing of the armistice with France on June 22, 1940, was a personal triumph for Hitler. From the start of his political career in the early 1920s, he had been motivated by a desire to avenge Germany's defeat in the First World War. Now he had achieved his goal, and France had been

A victorious Hitler stops in front of the Eiffel Tower during his sightseeing tour of Paris. At left is the Führer's favorite architect, Albert Speer. *The National Archives*

forced to accept terms as harsh as those it had once imposed on Germany. Half the country, including Paris, would be occupied by German troops. The other half (which came to be known as Vichy, after its seat of government) would be ruled by a government of French collaborators who were sympathetic to the Nazis. They promised to provide Germany with whatever it needed in the way of foodstuffs and other goods, including "volunteer" workers to labor in Germany's war plants.

To celebrate his triumph, Hitler planned a sightseeing tour of Paris, a city he had long admired but never visited. His favorite architect, Albert Speer, accompanied the Führer as he visited the ornate Paris Opera, drove down the broad Champs Élysées, stopped at the Eiffel Tower, and lingered for a long time at the tomb of Napoleon Bonaparte. The three-hour tour through almost completely deserted streets—the French deliberately stayed away—ended on the heights of Montmartre, long known as a district for artists. Perhaps its narrow streets and outdoor cafés reminded Hitler of his youthful days in Vienna, when he himself had dreamed of being an artist.

As he gazed down at the great city, bathed in the warm sunlight of a June day, the Führer said: "I thank Fate to have seen this city whose magic atmosphere has always fascinated me." Then he turned to Speer and said, "Now your work begins. Paris is beautiful, but Berlin must be made more beautiful!"

Hitler had no way of knowing it that balmy afternoon, but his victory over France and tour of a conquered Paris would prove to be the high point of his life, and his career.

19 · WAR ON TWO FRONTS

BY THE FIRST OF JULY 1940, Hitler's Germany controlled all of Europe's Atlantic coastline from Norway in the north to the Spanish border in the south. Only Great Britain was left to fight on against the Nazis, and the English Channel, which separated Britain from German-occupied France, offered little in the way of protection. At its narrowest point the Channel is just twenty-one miles wide.

Many of Hitler's close associates urged him to follow up the conquest of France by crossing the Channel and invading England. A plan for such an invasion was drawn up and labeled "Operation Sea Lion." But Hitler held off on implementing it. "I do not want to conquer her [England]," he told a high official in the Foreign Office. "I want to come to terms with her, I want to force her to accept my friendship and to drive out the whole Jewish rabble that is agitating against me."

He failed to grasp that the new British leader, Winston Churchill, had no interest in negotiating with Germany from a position of weakness. Instead, Churchill was doing his best to prepare the British people for the struggle to come. In a speech over London radio on July 14, he said: "We await undismayed the impending assault. Perhaps it will come tonight. Perhaps it will come next week. Perhaps it will never come. . . . But be the ordeal sharp or long, or both, we shall seek no terms, we shall tolerate no parley. We may show mercy—but we shall ask for none."

President Franklin D. Roosevelt supported Churchill's position. In a radio broadcast to the American people from the White House, he declared that the only way to deal with a totalitarian country like Germany was by resistance, not appeasement. Many people in the United States, including the heroic pilot Charles A. Lindbergh, opposed any American involvement in the European conflict. But Roosevelt overrode their opposition and promoted the Lend-Lease Act. This bill provided material aid in the form of ships, airplanes, munitions, and food to countries like Great Britain whose defense was considered vital to the defense of the United States.

Hitler, frustrated in his desire for negotiations with Britain and fearful of greater U.S. involvement in the war, backed off for a moment to consider his options. In that summer of 1940, he drew closer to Eva Braun. Although they still did not appear in public as a couple, and she was not introduced to important guests, Eva now occupied a suite close to Hitler's in Berlin's Reich Chancellery. She was also treated with respect by the servants and staff at the Berghof, the Führer's retreat in the Alps. When he and she relaxed there with friends, Hitler would sometimes

Hitler and Eva Braun in his Reich Chancellery apartment with Eva's niece, Uschi Schneider. *The National Archives*

call her a pet name or pat her hand in a show of affection—something he had never done before.

In August 1940, with Operation Sea Lion stalled, the Führer gave his approval to an all-out air assault on England by Göring's Luftwaffe. Perhaps that would bring the British to their knees and persuade the defiant Churchill to negotiate a peace treaty with Germany. Hitler and Göring were unaware that the British had broken Germany's top-secret military code, and thus knew in advance when and where the Luftwaffe's planes would strike.

The air campaign began on August 13, when more than 500 German bombers flew over the Channel, heading for military and industrial targets throughout southern Britain. But many of them never reached their destinations. British fighter pilots, alerted by warnings from the codebreakers, swept down on the heavy German bombers and knocked forty-five of them out of the sky. Only thirteen British planes were downed in the skirmishes.

This pattern was repeated in the days that followed. For every plane the British lost, the Germans usually lost three. The Luftwaffe switched from daytime to night raids, hoping to reduce the number of planes shot down, but British radar and antiaircraft fire proved surprisingly effective. And when German planes, during a night raid, strayed off course and dropped their loads on residential areas in London, the British retaliated by mounting their first bombing raid on Berlin.

The American correspondent William L. Shirer, reporting from the German capital, described the reaction to the raid: "The Berliners are stunned. They did not think it could happen. When the war began, Göring assured them it couldn't. He boasted that no enemy planes could ever break through the outer and inner rings of the capital's antiaircraft defense. The Berliners . . . believed him. Their disillusionment today therefore is all the greater."

The German attacks on London and other British targets grew more intense, and so did Britain's retaliatory raids on Berlin. Hitler found himself forced to respond. In a speech to women social workers and nurses on September 4, he brought the audience to its feet with these words: "When they [the British] declare that they will increase the attacks on our cities, then we will raze their cities to the ground. We will stop the handiwork of these air pirates, so help us God! The hour will come

Firemen in London battle a blaze after a German air raid in late August 1940.
The National Archives

when one of us will break, and it will not be National Socialist Germany!"

The audience answered the Führer by chanting, "Never! Never!" They—and he—conveniently forgot that Germany, not Britain, had been the first to launch nightly air raids on its opponent.

The raids on England continued, becoming fiercer by the day. London's East End, home of many of the city's poor, was badly battered, and historical landmarks like Coventry Cathedral near Birmingham were reduced to burned-out shells. But Prime Minister Churchill managed to rally the British people and lift their spirits. In his speeches, and in visits to bombed-out areas, Churchill made each man, woman, and child feel as if they were essential players in the struggle to save their nation.

By September 17, Hitler realized that the air campaign against Great Britain had failed. Neither the British government nor the country's economic structure had been seriously weakened, and Britain's army and air force had not suffered irreparable damage. True, the Royal Air Force had lost 915 fighter planes, but it had shot down almost 2,700 Luftwaffe bombers. Originally, Hitler had hoped that victory in the skies over England would pave the way for a land invasion of the British Isles that fall. Now he not only called a halt to the daily air attacks on England, but he and his generals also postponed Operation Sea Lion until the spring of 1941.

Before making further moves, Hitler decided it was time to put Germany's alliances with Italy and Japan on an even firmer footing. In late September, a Tripartite Pact among the three powers was signed in Berlin. The terms of the pact provided that Japan would recognize the leadership of Germany and Italy in Europe, and they would recognize Japan's leadership in Asia. The three countries also agreed "to assist one another with all political, economic, and military means" if one of the three was attacked by "a power at present not involved in the European war" or in Japan's ongoing conflict with China. The latter provision referred chiefly to the United States. As things turned out, it would be invoked sooner than either of the two European signers of the Tripartite Pact may have anticipated.

With the pact in hand, Hitler felt free to focus on two of his long-standing goals—the acquisition of more territory for Germany, and the destruction of Communism. If he moved against his so-called ally, the Soviet Union, there was a good chance that he could achieve both goals with one decisive blow. Defeat of the Soviet Union would also remove from the scene Britain's last hope for a European ally, and would make it easier for Germany to invade and conquer the British Isles when the time was right. In light of all this, the Führer ordered his generals to plan for a surprise attack on the Soviet Union in May 1941.

The generals countered by pointing out the risks involved in trying to wage a two-front war in both the east and the west. Hitler dismissed their concerns, arguing that an early attack on the Soviet Union would outweigh any possible risks. His greatest fear, he said, was that the United

States, which had begun to build up its armed forces, would enter the war on the side of Britain, and the Soviet Union would join forces with them. Better to strike now, when time was on Germany's side. For if the Soviet Union was out of the picture, the United States might think twice about getting into the war.

Hitler won over the generals, and together they settled on a code name for the Soviet invasion: "Operation Barbarossa." The name referred to Frederick Barbarossa, the Holy Roman Emperor who led his army east in 1190 to free the Holy Land from the Muslims. Germany's invasion plans had to be set aside momentarily when Italy suddenly launched a surprise attack on Greece. Stung by Hitler's victories in Scandinavia and western Europe, and Italy's unsuccessful invasion of southern France, Mussolini wanted to rack up some victories of his own.

The Italian attack soon ran into serious trouble, however. The Greeks put up an unexpectedly fierce resistance, and the British sent troops from Egypt, where they had military bases, to support the Greek cause. Hitler could not permit an Italian defeat in Greece and the establishment of a permanent British foothold there. The only way to prevent that from happening was to send German troops to reinforce Mussolini's battered army. But the mountainous land of Yugoslavia stood in the way and would have to be dealt with first.

When he could not come to an agreement with Yugoslavia, Hitler ordered a swift assault on that country, to be followed by an invasion of Greece. The German attack began on April 6, 1941, and quickly overcame all opposition. Yugoslavia surrendered on April 17, and Greece fell to the Germans six days later. The British expeditionary force fought bravely alongside the Greeks, but they were heavily outnumbered by the German invaders. In the end, the British managed to get most of their troops back to Egypt, but not before they had suffered heavy casualties.

Although they were victorious, the Germans suffered a loss of a different kind—one that would prove decisive in the long run. Originally, Hitler had planned to launch his invasion of the Soviet Union in May. That would have given his armies five months to advance into Russia and—if all went well—capture the capital, Moscow, before the harsh Russian winter set in. Now, because of the war in Yugoslavia and Greece, the date for the invasion had to be pushed back to June 22. But Hitler remained optimistic. He was convinced that the Nazi Blitzkrieg would sweep rapidly across the plains of western Russia and win a final victory within three months at the most. His generals were even more optimistic—so much so that they had ordered winter clothing for only one in five German soldiers.

Not everyone in Hitler's inner circle was in favor of the invasion, however. Some continued to warn of the dangers involved in attacking the Soviet Union in the east while waging war against Great Britain in the west. The most prominent of the naysayers, and the one closest to the Führer, was Rudolf Hess. Hitler had dictated *Mein Kampf* to Hess when both men were in prison following the beer-hall putsch, and Hess had served as the Führer's chief aide since 1933. In 1939, Hitler had named his old friend second in line of succession after Göring. Now Hess felt drastic action was needed to prevent the Führer from making a terrible mistake—and Hess believed he was the only one who could do it.

Hess was an experienced pilot who had flown in combat during World War I and had won several air races in the postwar years. Now, through a friend in the German aircraft industry, he obtained a small plane, and on May 10, without telling anyone, he took off on a secret mission to Great Britain. He planned to fly to Scotland, land by parachute on the estate of a prominent Englishman, the Duke of Hamilton, and tell the Duke he had come to Great Britain to begin negotiating a peace treaty between Britain and Germany. He would make it clear he was acting on his own, Hess told Hitler in a letter he left behind. If his attempt to achieve peace failed, Hitler would not be blamed. But if it succeeded, he would give all the credit to the Führer.

Hess arrived without incident over Scotland and parachuted safely to land near the Duke of Hamilton's estate. His plane crashed in a field close by. But Hess didn't meet the Duke—at least not right away. Instead, he was found by a farmer who took him to a local police station. Meanwhile, back in Germany, Hitler let out a shout after reading Hess's letter: "Oh, my God, my God! He has flown to England!" The Führer demanded to know if Hess had a chance of getting there in his small plane, and was told it wasn't likely. "I hope he falls into the sea," the Führer muttered, fearful that Hess might reveal the plans for Operation Barbarossa.

As the day wore on and no word came from Britain, Goebbels drafted an announcement to be broadcast over German radio. The communiqué

Rudolf Hess.
The National Archives

said that Hess had seized a plane against orders and disappeared. It was assumed that he had crashed. By way of explanation, the announcement said that Hess had left behind a letter that "showed traces of a mental disturbance which justifies the fear that Hess was a victim of hallucinations."

Goebbels had to revise this communiqué an hour or two later, after the British confirmed that Hess had, in fact, landed in Scotland. But the British provided no further details, leaving it to the Germans to guess what was happening with Hess, and what he might be telling his captors.

Martin Bormann. *The National Archives*

Hitler, in a meeting with regional German leaders, said that Hess's flight was "sheer insanity." The Führer went on to denounce Hess as a deserter, saying, "If I ever catch him, he will pay for this like any ordinary traitor!" Martin Bormann, who had been Hess's second-in-command, replaced his former boss on the Führer's staff and removed every trace of Hess from his office.

In England, Hess was telling his questioners that he had made his flight without Hitler's permission. He said nothing about Operation Barbarossa. Instead, he insisted that his only goal was "to convince responsible persons that since England could not win the war, the wisest course was to make peace now." But Prime Minister Churchill and other British leaders were not interested in Hess's proposals. On the night of May 16, Hitler's third in command was secretly transported to the Tower of London, where he became England's most prominent prisoner of war.

As the days passed, Hitler's attitude toward Hess softened. He told a close associate that he respected Hess's courage in undertaking such a dangerous mission and realized that his former aide had meant well. The Führer didn't think Hess was crazy, he said, only foolish to believe he could persuade the British to enter into peace negotiations. Meanwhile, Hitler and his generals moved full speed ahead with plans for the invasion of the Soviet Union. Three million soldiers were shifted from Germany and western Europe to new positions along the Polish-Russian border. With them came thousands of tanks, heavy artillery, and military aircraft.

These troop movements were obvious to many journalists and diplomats, and British codebreakers had even discovered the exact date of the invasion: June 22. They tried to warn Stalin and other Soviet leaders of Hitler's intentions, but their warnings were ignored. The Soviet dictator trusted the British even less than he trusted Hitler. Despite the mounting evidence, he was convinced that Great Britain only wanted to stir up trouble between the Soviet Union and Germany.

The German people were solidly behind their Führer as the date for the invasion neared. Some families had lost loved ones in the fighting in Poland, western Europe, and Greece, but their grief was outweighed by the pride Germans felt in the victories their armies had won. That pride in Germany's newfound strength made up for many of the privations brought on by the war—the shortages of such foods as meat, butter, and fruit, and the occasional air raids on German cities. In the eyes of most Germans, Adolf Hitler was responsible for making them feel proud once more, and they were willing to follow him wherever he wanted to lead them.

As for Hitler himself, he had begun to believe his own propaganda. He might still suffer from stomach upsets and sleepless nights, but he confided in one Nazi commander that he felt as if he had evolved into a "superhuman state" so that he was now "more godlike than human." Such an attitude made it harder than ever for even his most trusted colleagues to differ with him. It also hardened Hitler's conviction that he, and only he, was capable of deciding how best to fight the war.

On the evening of June 21, the commanders of the army units lined up along the Russian border read their men a special message from Hitler. "German soldiers!" it began. "You are about to join battle, a hard and crucial battle. The destiny of Europe, and future of the German Reich, the very existence of our nation, now lie in your hands alone."

At three A.M. on June 22—exactly a year after France had surrendered to Germany—the night sky was suddenly lit with flashes of artillery fire, and German infantrymen surged across the Russian border. The invasion of the Soviet Union had begun.

20 · THE "FINAL SOLUTION"

N EWS OF THE INVASION of the Soviet Union aroused a wide range of reactions at home and abroad. Joseph Goebbels reassured the German people by saying that Hitler estimated the invasion would last no more than three months. He himself, he said, believed the fighting would be over in eight weeks.

Caught off guard, the Soviet Premier, Joseph Stalin, thought at first that the invasion must be a mistake. Lacking firm leadership, the Soviet army retreated on a broad front, losing 1,200 aircraft in the process. The British Prime Minister, Winston Churchill, pledged that Britain would give Russia "the utmost help" in its struggle against the Nazis. Although he had no love for Soviet Communism, President Franklin D. Roosevelt agreed with Churchill that Hitler's Germany was a far greater evil. In answer to a reporter's question, Roosevelt said, "Of course we are going to give all the aid we possibly can to Russia."

Hitler's confidence was not shaken by the western leaders' words. On June 23, he left Berlin on his special train, headed for the Wolf's Lair, his new field headquarters in East Prussia. From there he and his generals would direct the course of the Russian campaign. "We have only to kick in the door, and the whole rotten structure will come crashing down," the Führer said, speaking of the Soviet Union. And for a time his prophecy seemed to be correct. By July 3, the German Wehrmacht had advanced deep into Russia and taken almost half a million prisoners. "To all intents and purposes the Russians have lost the war," a jubilant Hitler told his aides.

In August, the Führer issued an order outlining the future course of the Russian campaign. One German army would head north and seize the key

German troops sweep into the Soviet Union in 1941. *AP Wide World Photos*

industrial city of Leningrad (now Saint Petersburg), where the Russian Revolution had begun. Another army would move south into the Ukraine, the most important agricultural region in the Soviet Union, and capture its largest city, Kiev. Once these goals had been achieved, the central German army would drive straight toward Moscow, the Soviet capital.

Leningrad put up a fierce resistance to the German forces that blockaded the city, but Kiev surrendered to the Germans on September 17.

Now the way was clear, Hitler said, to occupy the rest of the Ukraine and move on south and east to the rich oil fields of the Caucasus. But first would come the attack on Moscow. Several of Hitler's generals warned that it was too late in the season to launch an attack on the Soviet capital. Why not spend the winter in fortified positions, then march against Moscow in the spring?

The Führer would hear none of that. Hadn't he promised the German people that the Soviet Union would be conquered in three months? Well, almost three months had passed, and he was not about to hold back now. "In several weeks we will be in Moscow," he said to his generals at the Wolf's Lair. "There is no doubt of it. Then I will raze that damned city. . . . The name of Moscow will disappear forever!" And so, on the last day of September, sixty-nine German divisions, supported by a vast number of tanks and fleets of military aircraft, moved east toward the Soviet capital.

At first the Germans seemed destined to achieve a swift victory. On October 6, two large Soviet army units were encircled near Bryansk. In Moscow, Stalin had not appeared in public for several days, and rumors were spreading that he had lost his nerve or fled to the east. Workers hastily erected barricades on the western outskirts of the capital as the German army drew ever closer. Some residents, resigned to a Nazi occupation, bought Russian-German dictionaries so that they would be able to say a few words to their conquerors. At dinner in Berlin on October 17, Hitler assured his guests that the Russian campaign would be over in a matter of days.

The Führer spoke too soon. Stalin reappeared in Moscow on October 19 and rallied the Soviet government and people in defense of the capital. Soviet troops successfully halted the German advance, which had reached a point just forty miles west of Moscow. And then the fall rains came, followed at the end of the month by sleet and the first snow of the season. The treads of Hitler's heavy tanks sank into the thick mud on the roads and refused to budge. Low clouds and freezing rain grounded the Luftwaffe's fighter planes and bombers. The German soldiers, many of whom lacked winter uniforms and boots, shivered and fell ill in subfreezing temperatures.

Although Hitler admitted to the Japanese ambassador that it was doubtful Moscow could be taken that year, he ordered that the offensive against the Soviet capital be continued. Early in December, a German advance party reached the western outskirts of Moscow and sighted the spires of the Kremlin in the city center. But a Soviet army detachment drove the Germans back, and by December 5, the temperature in the Moscow region had dropped to minus thirty-one degrees Fahrenheit. The Germans had to light fires under their tank engines to get them started. The wounded froze to death in unheated hospital tents, and soon the German casualties from the cold outnumbered those from the fighting.

Faced with desperate reports from the front, Hitler was forced to change his tactics. On December 6, he drafted a new directive to his generals. It began with an unusually frank summary of the situation: "The severe winter weather, which has come surprisingly early in the east, and the consequent difficulties in bringing up supplies, compel us to abandon immediately all major offensive operations and to go over to the defensive." Unlike the Führer's earlier statements, this new directive offered no definite timetable for victory in Russia. The directive was issued on December 7, 1941, just as Hitler received word of the Japanese attack on the U.S. naval base at Pearl Harbor in the Hawaiian Islands.

At first the Führer was elated by Japan's entry into the war. "Now we have a partner who has not been defeated in three thousand years!" he exclaimed to an aide. But at the same time he was fully aware of the threat that the United States, with its immense industrial capacity, posed to Germany. How different the situation would have been if, as planned, he had been able to defeat the Soviet Union before the Japanese attacked Pearl Harbor. Then Germany, Japan, and Italy would have confronted only a weakened Great Britain and a United States that was not yet prepared for all-out war.

Now, however, if Germany honored its treaty obligations to Japan and declared war on the United States, it would have to deal with three determined opponents: the United States, Great Britain, and a Soviet Union that had suddenly recovered its fighting will. Still, Hitler felt Germany must stand by Japan, one of its closest allies. And so on December 11, 1941, he convoked the Reichstag to announce that Germany was "at war with the United States, as of today."

While the German people were still absorbing this news, word came from the Soviet Union of new reverses on the Moscow front. Fresh troops from Siberia launched a counteroffensive that pushed the Germans

"Dividing Up the World." A still from a U.S. government filmstrip, "The Fruits of Aggression," made after Japan bombed Pearl Harbor and entered the war on the side of Germany and Italy. *The National Archives*

decisively back from the capital. The plains to the west of Moscow were littered with the abandoned tanks, field artillery, and trucks that the Germans had been forced to leave behind. Not since the Munich beer-hall putsch had Hitler experienced such a severe setback to his plans.

His exhausted generals urged Hitler to approve a further withdrawal. They argued that the army's supply lines were stretched to the limit and that many of the soldiers still lacked winter underwear and heavy woolen overcoats. Hitler refused even to consider a withdrawal. "You stand too close to the events," he told General Heinz Guderian. "You have too much pity for the soldiers." Instead, on December 16, he issued a general order demanding that the troops put up a determined resistance in their present positions despite any enemy breakthroughs. "Stand fast, not one step back!" the order concluded.

When several of his generals objected to the order, Hitler fired them on the spot and assumed personal command of the army. "Anybody can handle operational leadership—that's easy," he declared to a colleague. "The commander-in-chief's job is to train the army in the National Socialist idea, and I know of no general who could do that as I want it done. Therefore I have decided to take over command of the army myself." From then on, the Führer would bear the responsibility for the German army's victories—and for its defeats as well.

In January 1942, while the Russian front was comparatively quiet and the United States was defending the Philippine Islands against Japanese invaders, Reinhard Heydrich, the SS leader, convened a conference in Wannsee, a suburban section of Berlin. Its purpose: to decide on "the Final Solution of the Jewish question." One of Heydrich's key aides, Adolf Eichmann, organized the conference and took the official minutes of the meeting. Hitler did not attend the conference, and there was no indication that he had had a role in planning it. Still, it's almost certain that the Führer was behind the gathering, for it dealt with one of his major concerns—the ultimate fate of Europe's Jews.

Already the majority of German and Polish Jews had been crowded into ghetto areas in Poland's major cities. Those who were able to work labored in factories that made spare parts, boots, uniforms, and other goods for the German army. Like the rest of the ghettos' inhabitants, the workers barely survived on near-starvation rations. But even though they made a significant contribution to the German war effort, their contin-

Reinhard Heydrich, spokesman
for the "Final Solution."
The National Archives

ued existence rankled Hitler and his fellow Nazis. In *Mein Kampf,* the
Führer had envisioned a "racially pure" Europe, from which all Jews had
been removed. Now the Wannsee Conference had been convened to find
a way to achieve that goal.

Earlier, Hitler had talked vaguely of shipping the Jews to someplace in
"the East," or even deporting them to the French-controlled island of
Madagascar in the Indian Ocean, off the coast of Africa. A far more bru-

tal approach was employed during the invasion of the Soviet Union. Special-duty groups from the SS followed closely on the heels of the Wehrmacht, their members entrusted with a deadly mission. In each Soviet village they came to, the special-duty troops rounded up all the Jews who lived there and marched them out into the countryside, along with the Communist leaders of the community. There, without any trial or other proceeding, the Jewish and Communist prisoners were forced to dig a ditch. Then they were lined up and shot, their corpses falling backward into the ditch they had just dug.

None of these approaches seemed like a realistic way of dealing with all of Europe's 6 million Jews, however. At the Wannsee Conference, Heydrich laid out another possibility. While representatives from the army, the SS, the state police, and the government listened intently, he described how the Jews would be told that they were being "resettled." Instead, they would be transported on freight trains from their ghetto homes to concentration camps, where about 10 percent of the healthiest adults would be selected to work in factories attached to the camps. The remaining 90 percent—the old, the ill, the young—would be led off to what they thought were showers, but which were actually large, specially constructed gas chambers. There they would be gassed to death, and their bodies cremated.

Judging by transcripts of the conference proceedings, no one present raised any serious objections to Heydrich's proposal, which had obviously been approved in advance by the Führer. Adolf Eichmann was put in charge of organizing and scheduling the deportations, and he set to work at once. In March 1942, the first Jews from the Polish city of Lublin were transported to the Belzec camp, and a large party of Slovakian Jews arrived at Auschwitz. Thus began what would become known as the Holocaust.

Hitler never commented publicly on the new policy, but in a lunchtime conversation with Himmler and other Nazis on January 23, he had seemed to refer to it. Speaking of the Jews, the Führer said, "One must act radically. When one pulls out a tooth, one does it with a single tug, and the pain quickly goes away. The Jews must clear out of Europe. . . . For my part, I restrict myself to telling them they must go away. But if they refuse to go voluntarily I see no other solution but extermination."

While the "Final Solution" was being put into effect in the spring of 1942, Hitler focused his attention once more on the Russian front. The latest casualty figures depressed him: 199,448 German soldiers killed, 708,351 wounded, and 44,342 missing since the start of the campaign in June 1941. But, acting on his orders, the army had managed to hold on to its forward positions through the winter, and now fresh troops were on their way to the front. Most of the reinforcements came from Germany, but there were also divisions from its allies: Italy, Hungary, and Romania.

With the arrival of spring, Hitler moved to a new base deep in the Ukraine that he christened Werewolf. There he and his generals made plans for a summer offensive. The generals advised him to postpone any further assault on Moscow and concentrate the army's efforts instead on a swift drive east and south to the Caucasus. Seizure of that region's rich

Hitler's empire in the summer of 1942.

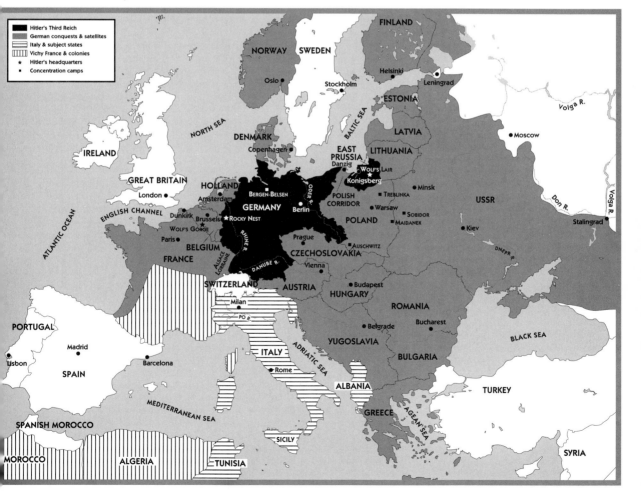

oil fields would provide Germany with a steady diet of the fuel it needed for its war machine.

Hitler agreed that the Caucasus should be a major target, but at the same time he wanted to push eastward to the industrial city of Stalingrad (now Volgograd) on the Volga River. His generals warned him that by trying to take both the Caucasus and Stalingrad, he risked spreading the army too thin, but Hitler refused to listen to them. Convinced that the Soviets lacked the resources to mount a counterattack, he insisted that the army move forward in both directions.

At first the Führer's instincts seemed to be correct. The divisions aimed at the Caucasus made slow progress through the mountain passes leading to the Black Sea, but by late August those headed toward Stalingrad had reached the city's northern outskirts. Still, Hitler was not satisfied with the pace of the advance. He ignored the advice of his generals and replaced several who disagreed with him. At mealtimes, he ate alone in his room at the Werewolf outpost, accompanied only by his German shepherd dog, Blondi.

Feeling a need to reassure the German people, the Führer returned to Berlin at the end of September to deliver a major speech at the Sportpalast. In it, he foresaw victory in Russia and pledged that the German Wehrmacht would shortly take Stalingrad. As things turned out, he spoke too soon. The first signs of trouble did not appear on the Russian front, however; instead, they swelled up from the desert sands of North Africa.

Starting in 1941, one of Germany's most able generals, Erwin Rommel, had commanded a German-Italian army in North Africa. Now, in late 1942, Rommel's troops had advanced into British-dominated Egypt and were threatening to gain control of both the Nile River and the Suez Canal, the vital shipping route to India. When Hitler spoke in Berlin, it looked as if Rommel would be in Cairo, the capital of Egypt, by the end of the year. But then, at the end of October, the tide turned. Under the leadership of Lieutenant General Bernard Montgomery, the British mounted a major counteroffensive and handed Rommel's army a crushing defeat at the battle of El Alamein.

Rommel radioed Hitler, informing him of the army's plight. The Führer radioed back a stern message similar to the one he'd sent the general in charge of the advance on Moscow the year before: "In the situation in which you now find yourself, there can be no other consideration

The Führer with his beloved dog, Blondi. *The Library of Congress*

than to hold fast, never retreat, hurl every gun and every man into the fray. . . . You can show your troops no other way than that which leads to victory or death." Fortunately for his men, Rommel had already ordered a retreat before he received the Führer's message, and he chose not to cancel the order.

Hitler was furious when he heard that a retreat was in progress in Egypt. But by that time he had more important things to worry about.

General Erwin Rommel, commander of the German and Italian forces in North Africa. *The National Archives*

On November 7, word reached him that an American and British armada (armed fleet) had made a successful landing on the northwest coast of Africa. Meanwhile, in Stalingrad, the Soviet defenders were putting up a fierce resistance even as massive Soviet army buildups were taking place both to the north and south of the city. General Friedrich Paulus, commander of the German Sixth Army at Stalingrad, was informed of the buildup and, fearing entrapment, requested permission to retreat to the west.

Hitler vetoed the request at once. "No matter what happens, we must hold the area around Stalingrad," he wrote. By the time the Führer's order reached Paulus, it was too late to retreat anyway. On the morning of November 22, the northern and southern arms of the Soviet army joined forces, encircling Paulus's entire Sixth Army. More than 220,000 of Germany's finest soldiers, along with 1,800 big guns and more than 10,000 tanks, trucks, and other vehicles, were caught in a giant trap.

21 · STALINGRAD—AND AFTER

ITLER AND HIS GENERALS sought ways to deal with the Stalingrad crisis. Göring vowed that the Luftwaffe could keep Paulus's army supplied by air with food and other necessities. Hitler took Göring at his word and radioed Paulus to hold on "at all costs," promising the general that help was on the way. But on the first day of the airlift, the Soviets shot down twenty-two of the Luftwaffe's planes, and on the second day they blasted nine more out of the sky. Only a fraction of the badly needed supplies reached Paulus's men.

Hitler then ordered a relief column of 230 tanks to break through to the entrapped Sixth Army. But those tanks that didn't get bogged down in the mud were halted by strong Soviet resistance. In the end, the general in charge of the relief column had no choice but to call off the effort. Meanwhile, an ever-more-desperate Paulus requested permission to stage a breakout attempt of his own. He told the Führer he had a mere 100 tanks at his disposal, and only enough fuel to travel twenty miles, but he still felt there was a good chance he could save most of his men. Hitler's reply: Stand fast in your present positions.

Early in January 1943, the Soviets launched a fresh attack on the Sixth Army and slowly pushed it back into an even smaller area. By now Paulus's men had very little ammunition left, and almost no food. Each soldier received just one slice of bread daily, along with a little horse meat. At the Führer's urging, the German airlift managed to improve its performance and get eighty tons of supplies a day through to Paulus's army. But that was still far from enough, and a feeling of hopelessness spread among the German soldiers. There was no place to put the newly wounded, for all the cellars of Stalingrad were already filled to bursting.

And graves for the dead could no longer be dug in the frozen ground.

Moved by the plight of his men, Paulus made a final appeal to Hitler. Soon the Sixth Army would no longer be able to carry on the fight, he wrote. When that time came, he requested permission to surrender in order "to avoid complete annihilation."

The Führer would hear none of it. "Surrender out of the question," he radioed General Paulus. "Troops will resist to the end." To reward Paulus for his steadfastness, Hitler promoted him on January 30 to the rank of field marshal.

The promotion came too late, however. When the new field marshal awoke on the morning of January 31, he discovered that his hungry, freezing troops had begun to surrender to the Soviets on their own. Unless he was willing to fire on his own men, there was nothing for Field Marshal Paulus to do but surrender also. And this he did later that day.

Two German soldiers surrender to the Russians at Stalingrad. *AP Wide World Photos*

A long line of German officers and soldiers march across a snowy hill to a prison camp after being captured by the Soviet army at Stalingrad.
AP Wide World Photos

On February 1, Moscow radio announced the surrender. It reported that more than 100,000 German soldiers had been captured, including 24 generals and 2,500 other officers. When he heard the news, Hitler had nothing good to say about Paulus. "How easy he has made it for himself!" the Führer exclaimed. "The man should have shot himself, as generals used to fall upon their swords when they saw that their cause was lost. . . . How can anyone be so cowardly? I don't understand it. What hurts me the most personally is that I promoted him to field marshal. I wanted to give him that last pleasure. That's the last field marshal I appoint in this war!"

Before Stalingrad, it was still conceivable that Adolf Hitler might lead Germany to victory in Europe. But after the surrender of Paulus's army—and the almost simultaneous German retreat in North Africa—the Nazis never really regained the initiative. However, the Führer was no more ready to accept this situation than he had been to accept the loss of Stalingrad. He had made his position clear in a speech he gave a few months earlier, in November 1942. "In me they [the Allies] are facing an opponent who does not even think of the word capitulate. It was always my habit, even as a boy, to have the last word. And let all our enemies take note. The Germany of the past [meaning the Germany of the First World War] laid down its arms before the clock struck twelve. I make it a principle not to stop until the clock strikes thirteen!"

Such defiance was all well and good, but Joseph Goebbels realized that the German people needed an outlet for their grief. Almost every family had experienced the loss of a loved one or friend in the Russian campaign. In mid-February, Goebbels proclaimed a three-day mourning period to honor those who had died at Stalingrad. He followed it with a call for all-out mobilization of the civilian economy and further sacrifices by the German people. To promote the mobilization, a new slogan appeared in shop windows and on billboards throughout the country: "The Wheels Must Turn Only for Victory!"

Apparently this campaign did not apply to the privileged few who traveled aboard Hitler's special train. It was always available to carry the Führer from Berlin to Berchtesgaden, or to one of his frontline outposts such as the Wolf's Lair. Unlike Germany's crowded civilian trains, which were operating without heat or food service because of the war, Hitler's train was supplied with hard-to-get meats, fruit, and pastries. The seats could be transformed into comfortable beds at night, and a special car was equipped with bathtubs, showers, and plenty of hot water.

Life was just as comfortable at the Berghof, Hitler's mountain retreat at Berchtesgaden. From his youth on, the Führer had always been a night person, and the pattern continued in the war years. Hitler rose a little before noon, ate a light breakfast, and then received a briefing on the military situation from his top officers. Following the briefing, he joined Eva

Hitler bends down to kiss Eva Braun's hand at his Berchtesgaden retreat.
The National Archives

Hitler and Eva Braun with their dogs on the terrace at Berchtesgaden, summer 1943. *The National Archives*

Braun and their guests for lunch, which was always served promptly at four in the afternoon.

Eva and the guests ate meat and sometimes sipped wine, but the Führer kept to a strict vegetarian diet prepared by his personal chef. A typical lunch of his consisted of vegetable soup, thick gruel, apple juice, and a baked potato soaked in linseed oil instead of butter. After lunch, Hitler led Eva and the guests on a walk down to the tea house, a small structure with a magnificent view of the Alps. Sometimes he had his dog, Blondi, perform tricks along the way for the guests' amusement.

At the tea house, beverages and pastries were served while Eva and the others chatted about movies and plays they'd seen. Hitler would sometimes complain that he could not watch a film while the German people were making so many sacrifices. "Besides, I must save my eyes for studying maps and reading frontline reports," he said as he drank a special tea made from apple peelings.

Hitler dozes after lunch while Eva Braun looks on.
The National Archives

At seven P.M., a long line of cars filled with aides would arrive at the Berghof, and the Führer would resume the business of running the government. Two hours later, at nine P.M., he'd leave the meeting to join Eva and the guests for a light supper. He ate mashed potatoes and maybe a tomato salad while the others dined on cold meats and stewed fruits. For the Führer, another military conference followed supper, but Eva and the guests often relaxed at a movie in the basement theater. Their day did not end with the movie, however. After the conference was over—usually around midnight—the Führer would summon Eva and the rest to join him in the living room for drinks and a snack.

Liquor was served, but Hitler limited himself to a cup of tea and perhaps a small slice of apple cake. Then everyone sat back and waited for him to take the lead in the conversation. Sometimes he lectured on the evils of smoking. "It is universally agreed that nonsmokers live longer than smokers and during sickness have more resistance," he would say. Or he might launch into a discussion of modern art and architecture, especially if Albert Speer was one of the guests. But one topic Hitler almost never discussed was the war; he didn't feel it was proper with ladies present.

As the night wore on, many of the guests found themselves fighting to stay awake. At last, around four A.M., the Führer would leave the room to study the latest air-raid reports, and the others would be free to go to their beds. As for Hitler, he said he could not rest until he had been assured that no enemy aircraft were still in the skies over Germany.

By the middle of 1943, it became harder and harder to keep the war out of the Führer's nightly conversations. There had been so many setbacks, one right after the other, and no relief was in sight. In early May, the Allies had closed in on the German-Italian army Rommel commanded in North Africa. Rommel managed to get away to Sicily with many of his men, but more than 300,000 prisoners and dead were left behind.

In July, Hitler and his generals mounted a fresh offensive at Kursk in central Russia. But the German soldiers were halted by fierce Soviet resistance, and the German tanks bogged down again in the thick mud of the Russian roads, impassable because of heavy rains. The Führer might have insisted on continuing the offensive anyway, but the deteriorating situation in the south forced him to change his plans. From North Africa, the Allies had launched an invasion of Sicily, the large Italian island in the middle of the Mediterranean Sea. Hitler transferred a German army division from Russia to Italy to help bolster the Italian position, but by mid-August, the Allies were in control of virtually all of Sicily.

Meanwhile, Italy's Fascist government had become disillusioned with Mussolini's leadership in the face of the country's military defeats abroad and food and fuel shortages at home. In late July, the Fascist Grand Council met in Rome and relieved Mussolini of his duties. The Council gave Italy's King, Victor Emmanuel III, command of the armed forces and asked Marshal Pietro Badoglio to organize a new government. Mussolini was arrested and jailed, and Badoglio began to negotiate an armistice with the Allies that would take Italy out of the war.

In early September, the Allies used newly conquered Sicily as a base from which to invade southern Italy. If Italy surrendered, the way would be open for the Allies to move north into Austria, and then into Germany itself. Hitler could not allow this to happen. He reinforced the already strong German military presence in central Italy and assigned General Rommel to take charge of the defense of northern Italy. Marshal Badoglio fled Rome for a new base in the southern part of the country, from which he continued to negotiate with the Allies. At this point, with Italy in a state of confusion, the Führer plotted a daring commando raid that freed Mussolini from his mountaintop prison. Then Hitler had the deposed Italian leader flown to Germany.

By now Mussolini's only goal was to retire, but Hitler had another future in mind for the former dictator. He wanted him to return to northern Italy and set up a new Fascist republic there with German backing. "The war must be won and once it is won Italy will be restored to her rights," the Führer said. "The fundamental condition is that Fascism be reborn and that the traitors be brought to justice." If Mussolini didn't agree to his plan, Germany would be forced to treat Italy as an enemy, the Führer concluded. The country would be occupied and governed entirely by Germans. To spare his people that fate, Mussolini at last agreed to do as the Führer wished.

Hitler had shored up the Italian front, at least for the moment. But to do so, he had had to transfer more troops from Russia, where they were just as sorely needed. The German newcomers fought bravely but were unable to prevent the British and American forces from advancing steadily up through Italy. On October 1, 1943, the Allies entered the city of

Naples, which the Germans had done their best to destroy before retreating northward.

The Germans were also retreating in Russia. Before the autumn ended, the Soviets had retaken such major cities as Smolensk, Kharkov, and Kiev. At the same time, Japan was experiencing serious setbacks in the Far East. Starting with the island of Guadalcanal, the American navy and air force was driving the Japanese slowly back across the vast Pacific Ocean, island by island.

Closer to home, the Allies' bombing of Germany intensified throughout 1943. One of the most severe air raids hit the key port city of Hamburg. In one night of firebombing, more than 6,000 acres of factories, office buildings, and homes were destroyed and 70,000 people were killed. When Hitler heard of the destruction, he stormed about his office claiming that British Jews must have been responsible for the raid.

The Jews were very much on Hitler's mind at the end of 1943. He might have lost control of the war, but he was still in complete charge of the "Final Solution." And just as the retreat from Moscow was followed by the Wannsee Conference that established the policy of extermination, so now, in the face of German defeats in Russia and Italy, the Führer and his associates decided to step up the pace of the killings. In September 1943, the ghettos of Minsk in Byelorussia and Vilna in Lithuania were liquidated; in October, the ghetto of Riga, Latvia, was wiped out and thousands of Jews from southern France were deported to Auschwitz. At the end of the year, more than 7,000 Jews from northern Italy were shipped to the death camps.

Apparently their executioners never questioned whether the Jews deserved such a horrible fate. "We were all so trained to obey orders, without even thinking, that the thought of disobeying an order would simply never have occurred to anybody," Rudolf Höss, the commandant of the Auschwitz camp, confessed later. "One of us would have shot his own brother if ordered to. Orders were everything."

Until the fall of 1943, Hitler and his fellow Nazis did their best to keep the gas chambers a secret from everyone who was not directly involved with their operation. But as the extermination policy took hold, it inevitably affected other aspects of life in wartime Germany. Many factory managers had come to depend on Jewish slave labor and did not know how they could meet their production quotas if all their Jewish workers

Young and old wait in line for soup in a Polish concentration camp.
The Library of Congress

were deported. Those responsible for running Germany's network of freight trains had a hard time fulfilling the needs of the soldiers at the front while at the same time transporting thousands of Jews to the death camps.

In order to explain the policy, Heinrich Himmler held a series of meetings with party and government leaders in the fall of 1943. (Himmler had assumed overall responsibility for the killing centers following the assassination of Reinhard Heydrich by Czech freedom fighters in 1942.) Carrying the "Final Solution" through to the end was a major priority of the Führer, Himmler said at one gathering, and he stressed that it must also be a priority of the entire nation. "The sentence 'The Jews must be exterminated' can be uttered easily," he said. "But what that sentence demands of the man who must execute it is the hardest and toughest thing in existence."

Himmler went on: "When the question arose, 'What should be done with the women and children?' I decided to adopt a clear solution. I did not deem myself justified in exterminating the men—that is to say, to kill them or have them killed—while allowing their children to grow up to avenge themselves on our sons and grandchildren." Himmler paused for emphasis. "The hard decision had to be made—*this people must disappear from the face of the earth.*"

One of those present, Baldur von Schirach, a leader of the Hitler Youth, was stunned by Himmler's speech. "He spoke," Schirach recalled later, "with such icy coldness of the extermination of men, women and children, as a businessman might speak of his balance sheet. There was nothing emotional in his speech, nothing that suggested an inner involvement."

When Himmler was finished, no one in the audience questioned anything he had said. Like the commandant of Auschwitz, they knew what was expected of them: Listen carefully to the Party leader, applaud him at the end of his remarks, and then carry out his instructions to the letter. But many of Himmler's listeners that day found another way to express their deeper feelings. When they joined him afterward at lunch, they made it a point to get drunk.

Christmas 1943 was a gloomy time for Hitler and Germany. The Italian front remained shaky, and the Soviet army was retaking area after area that it had previously lost to the Germans. In some sections, the Soviets had advanced more than 250 miles in the past six months. Hitler did not like to hear bad news from the front, but he could not escape the reality of the latest casualty figures. More than 1,686,000 German soldiers had been killed, wounded, or captured in 1943 alone, and replacements for them were so hard to find that fifty-year-old men, veterans of the First World War, were now being drafted.

Despite nightly bombing raids and the loss of loved ones in the fighting, most Germans still expressed faith in their Führer. Some may have been motivated more by fear of the SS than by sincere belief, but even so they listened intently to every word of Hitler's radio broadcasts and cheered his rare public appearances. Behind the scenes, however, there was growing dissatisfaction with the way the Führer was handling the war. Many of his generals were troubled by his growing isolation, his refusal to listen to the opinions of others, and his insistence that he and he alone was capable of determining military strategy.

Some of those who questioned Hitler's leadership merely grumbled and complained in conversations with trusted associates. But as 1944 began, others started to plot actively against the Führer. Some of their plots were confined to various ways he might be removed from power so that negotiations to end the war could begin. But other opponents went much further. Fearing that even a powerless Hitler would be a threat to peace, they set in motion plans for his assassination.

22 · A BOMB UNDER THE TABLE

FROM THE TIME HITLER came to power, the SS and the secret police had kept a tight lid on protests against his rule. Punishments for even the most peaceful demonstrations were severe. A well-known Protestant minister, Martin Niemöller, was imprisoned from 1938 until 1945 merely for speaking out from his pulpit against the excesses of the Nazi regime.

Despite the risks involved, many courageous people in German-occupied Europe banded together to oppose Hitler and his policies. In France, Poland, Yugoslavia, the Soviet Union, and other countries, underground resistance groups sprang up everywhere. Members of these groups risked capture and death to blow up German troop trains, stage slowdowns in factories, and commit other acts of sabotage designed to hinder the German war effort.

In Germany itself, a group of students at a university in Munich dared in 1942 to criticize Hitler's conduct of the war. The group adopted the name the White Rose, symbolizing purity, and, with the aid of one of their professors, wrote, duplicated, and distributed leaflets attacking the Führer. A typical leaflet, headed "An Appeal to All Germans," stated boldly that the war was lost and urged its readers to part company with Hitler and his fellow Nazis.

"Prove by your actions that you think differently," the leaflet said. "Tear off the cover of indifference which you have put around your hearts. Make your decision before it is too late. Do not believe that Germany's future is associated for better or worse with the victory of National Socialism. Criminal actions can never obtain a German victory." The leaflet concluded with a vision of the future. "Freedom of speech, freedom

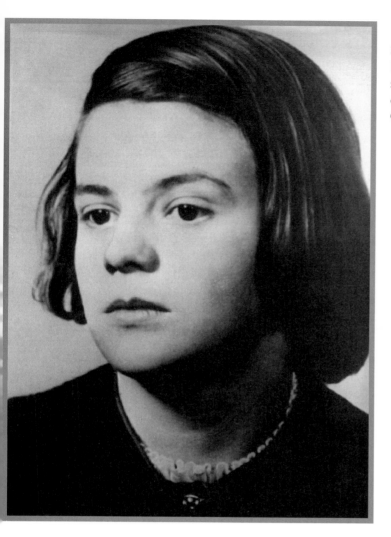

Sophie Scholl, one of the leaders of the White Rose student group that opposed Hitler.
Corbis/Bettman

of religion, protection of the individual citizen from the arbitrary actions of criminal terror states—those are the foundations for a new Germany, a new Europe. Support the resistance movement and pass on the leaflets."

At first White Rose members distributed the leaflets only to their fellow students within the university. Then they branched out, stuffing the pamphlets into mailboxes throughout Munich and even traveling to other cities, such as Stuttgart, Frankfurt, and Vienna, with the leaflets concealed in their suitcases. Back in Munich, they were distributing a fresh batch at the university when a janitor spotted them and notified the police.

Put on trial for treason in February 1943, the three leaders of the White Rose—Hans Scholl, his sister, Sophie, and their good friend Christoph Probst—were all sentenced to death by beheading. The trio remained defiant to the end. Sophie walked to the guillotine with a smile on her face, and her brother Hans shouted, "Long live liberty!" before he died.

If Hitler had a reaction to the White Rose group, it was not recorded. Nor, apparently, did he and his inner circle know of the other resistance groups that were formed in the wake of the German defeat at Stalingrad. This was a tribute to the skill of the plotters in keeping their plans secret—an especially difficult task, since many of the organizers were high-ranking officers who had frequent contact with Hitler and other Nazi leaders. It would have been only too easy for one of them to let something slip by accident.

The plotters were united in the belief that Hitler must be removed from power so that an end to the war could be negotiated. But they did not agree on what should happen to the Führer after he was deposed. Some thought imprisonment would be enough, but the majority felt strongly that as long as Hitler lived, he would be a danger. They made plans to assassinate him by planting a time bomb at one of the meetings or events he was scheduled to attend. However, that proved to be more difficult than they had anticipated. The plotters' first attempt failed when a meeting with Hitler was canceled at the last minute, and the second when an Allied air raid broke up the gathering.

Many prominent army men were in sympathy with the plotters' efforts. The best-known was probably Field Marshal Erwin Rommel, who had recently been transferred from Italy to France so that he could organize the defense of western Europe against an expected Allied invasion. Rommel was one of those in favor of merely arresting the Führer, but another plotter, Colonel Claus von Stauffenberg, believed strongly that Hitler must be assassinated. Stauffenberg had originally been a staunch supporter of National Socialism and had lost his right eye, his right hand, and two fingers from his left hand while fighting for Germany in North Africa. But he had become totally disillusioned with Hitler after the disaster at Stalingrad.

Despite his injuries, Stauffenberg volunteered to lead the way in eliminating the Führer and establishing a new German government. He had already begun to lay plans for a fresh bombing attempt when something happened that made him halt his plans temporarily. On June 6, 1944, an Allied force made up of more than 175,000 soldiers swept across the English Channel and stormed the beaches of Normandy. At the same time, 1,200 tanks rumbled ashore while 12,000 British and American planes provided air cover. The long-expected Allied invasion of France had begun.

At first Hitler did not take the invasion seriously. He thought that it was merely a diversionary attack and that the real invasion would occur at another point along the French coast. But by nightfall the Allies, aided by French resistance fighters, had shattered the German shore defenses and begun to push inland. They were obviously in France to stay.

In retaliation, Hitler ordered the launching of a new weapon against London and other British targets. This was the V-1 rocket, a jet-engined buzz bomb that zoomed down out of the sky without warning. The V-1s destroyed many buildings in London and other cities and killed or wounded countless civilians. But the bombs did not have any direct impact on the military situation in France. Within ten days of the invasion, the Allies had managed to land almost a million soldiers and had achieved complete supremacy in the air.

On June 17, an anxious Hitler traveled to France for a meeting with his generals. As usual, the Führer insisted on a policy of no retreat, but Field Marshal Rommel told him bluntly that such a stand would be futile in the face of Allied strength. He brushed aside Hitler's argument that the new V-1 rockets would force the British to sue for peace and predicted that it would be impossible for the German army to defeat the Allies in the west while at the same time battling the Soviets in the east. Therefore, he urgently requested the Führer to negotiate an end to the war while Germany was still relatively strong.

This was not what Hitler wanted to hear. "Don't you worry about the future course of the war," he said angrily to Rommel. "Just look to your own invasion front." When he returned to Germany, the Führer was still in a bad mood. "Rommel has lost his nerve; he's become a pessimist," he told an aide. "In these times only optimists can achieve anything." But, knowing Rommel's abilities, he did not remove the general from his command.

Meanwhile, Colonel Stauffenberg and his fellow plotters stepped up their plans to assassinate Hitler. With the Allies steadily advancing in France, and President Roosevelt, Prime Minister Churchill, and Premier Stalin stating they would accept only an unconditional surrender from Germany, the plotters felt they had no time to waste. If they didn't move

Hitler gives instructions to General Erwin Rommel (right) at a meeting in France in June 1944. *The National Archives*

quickly, they might not be able to negotiate a peace treaty that was in any way favorable to Germany.

In early July, Colonel Stauffenberg outlined the assassination plan to his fellow conspirators. Stauffenberg often attended the Führer's daily conference at Wolf's Lair in East Prussia. The next time he was invited, he would plant a time bomb that would blow up Hitler and any other Nazi leaders who might be present. He himself would find a way to get out of the meeting room before the bomb went off. After confirming that the Führer was dead, he would fly back to Berlin and personally supervise the military takeover of the capital.

On July 18, Stauffenberg was asked to report to Wolf's Lair two days later, on the twentieth. At once the colonel set his plan in motion. On the nineteenth he had his trusted adjutant pick up a briefcase containing two bombs that had been prepared by another conspirator. Stauffenberg and his adjutant flew to an airfield near Wolf's Lair on the morning of the twentieth and had no trouble getting past the three security checkpoints on the road to Hitler's headquarters. As usual, their passes were examined carefully, but not the contents of the colonel's briefcase.

At Wolf's Lair, Stauffenberg sought out a staff officer, General Erich Fellgiebel, who was part of the plot. The officer, who was in charge of communications at the headquarters, had a key role to play. As soon as the bomb went off and Stauffenberg confirmed that the Führer was dead, Fellgiebel would notify the plotters in Berlin, who would proceed with their takeover of the army and government. Then, as Stauffenberg made

The Führer presides over a conference with Hermann Göring (left) and other aides at his Wolf's Lair headquarters in East Prussia, summer 1944.
AP Wide World Photos

his escape, Fellgiebel would cut all telephone and teleprinter lines from Wolf's Lair, making it impossible for Hitler's aides to communicate with the outside world.

After briefing Fellgiebel, Colonel Stauffenberg had to move swiftly. The conference with the Führer would begin in just thirty minutes. Saying he wanted a place to wash up and change his shirt, the colonel was directed to an officer's private room. There, with the help of his adjutant, he set the fuse in one of the bombs; it would go off in fifteen minutes. At this point someone called from the hall, "Come on, Stauffenberg! The Chief is waiting!" There was no time to set the fuse on the second bomb, so the adjutant stashed it in his own briefcase. Then Stauffenberg picked up the briefcase containing the active bomb and headed for the meeting room.

When the colonel entered the room, he saw that the conference was already under way. Hitler sat with his back to the door, studying a map that was spread out in front of him on a thick oak table. A general to Hitler's right was in the midst of a report about the worsening situation on the Russian front. Stauffenberg indicated to a guard that his hearing was impaired and asked to be seated close to the Führer so that he could hear everything that was said. He was ushered to a seat just beyond the general who was speaking.

Stauffenberg focused his good eye on the general while at the same time putting his briefcase under the table and shoving it in Hitler's direction with his foot. The bomb inside the case was due to explode in just five minutes. Stauffenberg listened to the general's report for a minute more, then got up as unobtrusively as possible and moved toward the exit. The Führer did not seem to notice. Stauffenberg explained to an officer guarding the door that he had forgotten something he needed for his report. He walked swiftly down the hall and joined his adjutant, who was waiting for him in an anteroom. Together they hurried toward the building where General Fellgiebel was on duty.

Promptly at twelve forty-two P.M., there came an explosion from the Führer's headquarters. Stauffenberg and Fellgiebel watched as a cloud of smoke rose from the building and pieces of wood and paper swirled up into the air. Assuming that the Führer was dead—how could he have survived such a blast?—they turned their attention to the next stage of the plot. Fellgiebel would get on the wire to those waiting for word in Berlin. Meanwhile, Stauffenberg would fly back to the capital and assume command of the takeover.

The colonel bluffed his way through the three checkpoints, and at one o'clock he and his adjutant climbed aboard their waiting plane and took off for Berlin. Stauffenberg relaxed in his seat, assuming that General Fellgiebel back at Wolf's Lair had let the plotters in Berlin know what had happened. But an unexpected hitch had developed. Immediately after the explosion, Hitler's own aides had ordered that all telephone and teleprinter lines be shut down until the situation could be clarified. Consequently, Fellgiebel had not been been able to contact Stauffenberg's fellow conspirators.

Meanwhile, as smoke continued to hover over Hitler's headquarters and ambulances arrived to take the wounded to the field hospital, it was still not clear exactly what had happened. One thing was certain, though: Hitler had not been killed. In fact, he wasn't even seriously injured. Just before the bomb went off, someone at the conference table had accidentally kicked Stauffenberg's briefcase farther away from the Führer. As a result, he had escaped the worst effects of the blast. His trousers were tattered, his face was blackened by soot, and his right elbow was severely sprained. But he was able to walk away from the wrecked conference room on his own.

"Think of it," Hitler exclaimed to Dr. Morell. "Nothing has happened to me. Just think of it!" Later, he expanded on his luck in talking with his secretaries. "Well, my ladies, once again everything has turned out well for me," he said. "More proof that Fate has selected me for my mission. Otherwise, I wouldn't be alive."

At first the Führer's aides thought foreign workers who were making repairs at Wolf's Lair had planted the bomb. But then someone remembered that Colonel Stauffenberg had put a briefcase under the conference table and then left the room. On checking further, the aides discovered that Stauffenberg had hurried to the airport and taken off for Berlin a little after one P.M.

When Hitler was told of Stauffenberg's actions, he became convinced that the colonel was behind the assassination attempt, and his voice rose in anger. "Traitors in the bosom of their own people deserve the most ignominious of deaths," he shouted. "And they shall have it!" He ordered Stauffenberg's arrest, but the order could not be carried out. The telecommunication lines to Berlin had not been restored yet.

At three forty-two P.M., Stauffenberg finally landed at a military airfield near Berlin. He was surprised that no one was there to meet him, and even more surprised when he phoned army headquarters and learned that the takeover plot had not been launched. His fellow conspirators, hearing nothing from Wolf's Lair, had decided to wait until Stauffenberg returned before moving forward with their plans.

Stauffenberg acted quickly to make up for lost time. He and his fellow plotters took control of central army headquarters in Berlin and sought to line up support from other groups in the capital. But the commander of the Berlin garrison was reluctant to join in the plot until he had definite confirmation that Hitler was dead. Unwilling to take Stauffenberg's word for it, the commander dispatched an aide to Goebbels's office. The Propaganda Minister's staff was as confused as everyone else in Berlin until a call came through from Wolf's Lair. Telephone communication had been reestablished and Hitler was on the line. He urged Goebbels to go on the radio at once to let the German people know that he, the Führer, was very much alive.

Goebbels's broadcast came as a great relief to most of his listeners. Despite the military setbacks the nation had suffered, the majority of Germans still believed in the Führer and depended on his leadership. At the same time, the broadcast severely weakened the conspirators' chances for success. Stauffenberg charged that the broadcast was a lie, a desperate attempt by Goebbels to cover up the truth about Hitler's death. But one by one the military leaders he had been counting on for support distanced themselves from the takeover plot. By ten-thirty that evening, Stauffenberg, his fellow plotters, and a few other officers were isolated in the central army headquarters building. At that point, eight of the officers, who secretly remained loyal to Hitler, turned on Stauffenberg and his associates and arrested them.

A hastily convened court-martial sentenced Stauffenberg and his comrades to death "in the name of the Führer." The condemned men were led down to the army building's inner courtyard and lined up in front of a pile of sand used to fight air-raid fires. The courtyard was lit eerily by

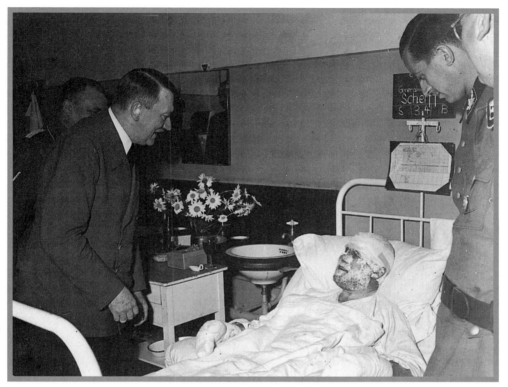

Hitler visits one of the men injured in the blast that was meant to kill him.
The National Archives

the headlights from several parked vehicles. By now it was midnight. As a marksman aimed his rifle, Stauffenberg shouted, "Long live our sacred Germany!" Then a shot rang out, ending the life of Hitler's would-be assassin.

The Führer himself addressed the nation by radio an hour or so later, at one in the morning. "I speak to you today for two reasons," Hitler said. "First, so that you may hear my voice and know that I am uninjured and well, and secondly, so that you may learn the details about a crime like no other in German history." He went on to describe the plot and the role played by Colonel Stauffenberg. "A very small clique of ambitious, wicked, and stupidly criminal officers forged a plot to eliminate me and virtually the entire leadership of the armed forces," the Führer said. "The group represented by these usurpers is ridiculously small. It has nothing to do with the German armed forces and above all with the German army. It is a tiny coterie of criminal elements which is now being mercilessly uprooted."

The German public was reassured by the Führer's words, but his statements proved to be overly optimistic—and not entirely accurate.

23 · THE LAST OFFENSIVE

HITLER SENT HIS TROUSERS that had been tattered in the explosion to Eva Braun in Berchtesgaden. He said in an accompanying note that he thought they would be a historical relic. He also sent Eva a sketch of the bombed headquarters building and assured her that he was feeling fine, although a bit tired. "I hope to come back soon and so be able to rest, putting myself in your hands. I greatly need tranquility."

That was an understatement. In the wake of the explosion, Hitler discovered that his injuries were more serious than anyone had realized. His right eardrum had been ruptured by the blast, making it difficult for him to hear in that ear; his right eye flickered constantly; and his right arm and hand trembled so violently that he could no longer shave himself. Besides these complaints, his old problem with stomach cramps had returned, and he suffered from insomnia. He told his doctors that he often got only two or three hours of sleep a night. The rest of the time he lay awake, brooding about the war and the attempt on his life.

New findings about the extent of the plot only made him feel worse. Himmler and Martin Bormann led a thorough investigation that ended with the arrest of more than 5,000 people who were suspected of having been involved. This figure included not just the suspects themselves but also members of their immediate families. Eight of the accused, all of them high-ranking officers, were brought before a people's court on August 7, 1944, and tried on charges of treason against the Führer. Among them was General Erich Fellgiebel, Stauffenberg's collaborator at Wolf's Lair.

The judge—who had also presided over the trial of the White Rose leaders—found all eight guilty and sentenced them to an unusually brutal form of death by hanging. Nooses of wire were placed around their

One of those accused of plotting to kill the Führer is interrogated by Judge Roland Freisler (left) before being sentenced to death. *The National Archives*

necks, and the condemned were hung from meathooks like slabs of beef. Goebbels's propaganda machine filmed both the trial and the executions as a warning to any other Germans who might be thinking of plotting against the Führer.

The role of the most prominent conspirator was not publicized, however. In October, Hitler learned that Field Marshal Erwin Rommel had supported the plot against him. Knowing how popular Rommel was among the German people, the Führer wanted to avoid bringing him to trial. Instead, he sent two representatives to the field marshal's home with an offer. If Rommel committed suicide by taking poison, he would be given a state funeral with all honors, and his family would not be harmed. But if he refused, he would be tried before a people's court, which would no doubt find him guilty and sentence him to death. And his wife and children would surely be persecuted.

Rommel really had no choice; he took the poison. The Führer did not attend his funeral, but he issued a statement on the same day. In it, Hitler repeated the official explanation that Rommel had died of severe wounds following an automobile accident. "With him, one of our best army leaders has passed away," Hitler concluded.

The Führer was furious with Rommel and the other army officers for having betrayed him. His anger even spilled over into his relationship with his dog, Blondi. That fall one of Hitler's secretaries overheard him disciplining the dog after she disobeyed him. "Look me in the eyes, Blondi!" the Führer said. "Are you also a traitor like the generals of my staff?"

Hitler could have used the services of Rommel and the other disgraced officers as he tried to deal with the military crisis that Germany faced in the last half of 1944. On August 15, the Allies landed in southern France and moved to join the other Allied forces that were sweeping across the northern part of the country. On August 24, the people of Paris celebrated their liberation after four years of Nazi occupation. The Allied armies kept on going, and on September 11 an American patrol for the first time crossed the border between France and Germany.

Meanwhile, in the east, the Soviet army occupied Bulgaria, a German ally, and seized Romania's oil fields, a vital source of fuel for the German military machine. Farther north, the Soviets fought their way across Poland and closed in on the capital, Warsaw. By the end of September, Soviet forces had reached Poland's prewar eastern border with East Prussia. They were now within striking distance of Hitler's outpost at Wolf's Lair.

As the Allied armies closed in on Germany itself, and Allied bombers pounded German cities nonstop, Goebbels and the other Nazi leaders took drastic steps to mobilize the population and prepare for the worst. On August 24, all theaters, concert halls, and nightclubs were closed. Every physically fit male between the ages of fifteen and sixty was drafted into the *Volkssturm* (People's Militia), and all women up to the age of fifty had to register for work in offices and factories. Younger members of the Hitler Youth were evacuated from the bombed-out cities and sent to live in rural villages and on farms.

Despite the incessant bombing, Albert Speer, boss of Germany's war industry, managed to maintain and even increase the output of military

A German woman tries to save her belongings during an Allied air raid.
The National Archives

equipment. The country's factories, staffed in large part by prisoners and forced laborers from France, Holland, Belgium, and other occupied countries, managed to produce more tanks and planes in 1944 than they had in 1943. But the loss of key sources of raw materials, such as Romanian oil, was felt more and more keenly. As 1944 came to an end, explosive materials like gunpowder were being stretched with up to 20 percent salt, and countless fighter planes sat uselessly on runways for lack of fuel.

While Germany's armed forces struggled to keep on waging war, the Führer was fighting his own battles with failing health. After the attempt on his life, Hitler hardly ever left his military headquarters. Walking was difficult for him, and he was frequently overcome by dizziness. His stomach cramps were almost constant now. To ease the pain, he took large quantities of the antigas pills that Dr. Morell prescribed, ignoring warnings that an overdose could be dangerous. In September, his memory began to deteriorate, and he had trouble remembering names. Later that month, he suffered several mild heart attacks.

Hitler's doctors saw the extreme stress that he was under and urged him to take an extended rest. He refused, saying, "I must work and think only of the German people day and night." His continuing obsession, though, was not the German people but the Jews. Even at this late stage in the war, with the fate of Germany itself in doubt, the Führer was preoccupied by his anti-Jewish campaign. As the Soviet army drew closer to the concentration camps and killing centers in Poland, he set aside his concerns about his health and asked for a progress report on the extermination program.

Adolf Eichmann declared that 6 million Jews had already been eliminated—4 million in the gas chambers of Poland and 2 million more in the mass killings that had been conducted in the Soviet Union. The Führer was not satisfied; many Jews remained alive in Hungary, Slovakia, Italy, and the occupied countries of western Europe. But he ordered Himmler to dismantle the Polish killing centers before the advancing Soviets discovered their existence. Only the gas chambers at Auschwitz would continue to function, Hitler said, and they should be able to finish the job—assuming the German troops fulfilled their mission of beating back the Soviets.

In late September, British and American troops moved into the hilly, thickly forested Ardennes region of Belgium, near the western border of Germany. At first Hitler assumed a defensive posture aimed at holding back the Allied armies as long as possible. But then he seemed to get a fresh burst of energy. He called his generals together and told them he had decided to take the offensive for the first time since the Allied invasion of Normandy. Before it began, there would be an army buildup along the Belgian border, conducted in complete secrecy. Then the army would wait for a spell of bad weather to ground the Allied air force before it launched a surprise attack.

The German shock troops, supported by tanks, would drive a wedge between the British and American forces in the Ardennes. Once that goal was accomplished, they would cross the Meuse River and fight their way through to the Belgian port of Antwerp, which the Allies depended on for supplies. The attack would be so startling and so devastating, Hitler said, that the British and Americans would be forced to sue for peace. Then Germany could turn all its attention toward fighting the Soviets.

The Führer's generals were wary of the plan, especially since it meant withdrawing troops from the Russian front to beef up the army in the west. But Hitler insisted that a dramatic move was necessary if Germany was to regain the initiative, and as usual he got his way. Firm plans were made for "Autumn Mist," the code name for the attack, and all possible army reserves were moved into place along Germany's border with Belgium and Luxembourg. More than 200,000 German troops backed by 600 tanks would face approximately 80,000 American soldiers equipped with 400 tanks.

To build morale among his commanders, Hitler decided to leave Wolf's Lair and travel west by train to Eagle's Nest, the base near Frankfurt from which he had directed the invasion of western Europe in the spring of 1940. He arrived on December 11 and spoke to half the commanders that afternoon; he met with the rest the following day. The Führer's aides took great pains to prevent any new attempt on his life. Everyone attending the meetings had to hand over his briefcase and revolver to SS men before entering the conference room. An armed bodyguard stood behind every chair, and one of the participants later said, "None of us would have dared even to pull out his handkerchief."

Hitler tried to make a strong impression, choosing to sit rather than stand so that those present would not see him wobble. Even so, one of the attendees described him as "a stooped figure with a pale and puffy face, hunched in his chair, his hands trembling, his right arm subject to a violent twitching which he did his best to conceal." Compared to the way he had looked just a few months earlier, the Führer struck this observer as "a man suddenly grown old."

His words were as forceful as ever, though. "The battle must be fought with brutality and all resistance must be broken," he said. "In this most serious hour of the Fatherland, I expect every one of my soldiers to be courageous, and then courageous again." He brought his fist down on the table. "The enemy must be beaten—now or never! Thus lives Germany!"

The attack was set to begin in the early hours of December 16, and at first all went well. The Germans caught the American soldiers facing them completely off guard. A big help to the Germans was the foggy, drizzly weather that kept all Allied planes on the ground. More than 8,000 American soldiers surrendered in the first two days of the battle, and the Germans completely surrounded another American division in the town of Bastogne. A newscaster on Radio Berlin predicted confidently, "We shall present the Führer with Antwerp for Christmas."

By December 21, the German attack had reached almost to the Meuse River and had assumed the shape that would give the venture its name— the Battle of the Bulge. But the invasion had peaked, although the Führer didn't know it yet. On the twenty-second, the skies cleared over the Ardennes, the sun came out, and hundreds of Allied planes took to the air. They dove down on the forward German positions and strafed the Nazis' supply lines. At the same time, a relief column was on its way to free the Americans trapped at Bastogne.

Once more Hitler summoned his commanders to Eagle's Nest, this time to urge them to hold on and not lose heart. He spoke in unusually personal terms. "Never in my life have I accepted the idea of surrender," he said, "and I am one of those men who have worked their way up from nothing. Our present situation, therefore, is nothing new to me."

He seemed to be recalling his impoverished youth in Vienna and Munich as he continued. "Once upon a time my own situation was entirely different, and far worse. I say this only so that you can grasp why I pursue my goal with such fanaticism and why nothing can wear me down." Then he returned to the present and indirectly referred to the recent attack on his life. "No matter how much I might be tormented by

A German soldier and his comrade carry ammunition boxes forward during the Battle of the Bulge, December 1944. *The National Archives*

worries, even if my health were shaken by them—that would still have not the slightest effect on my decision to fight on."

But the Führer's words alone could not shift the direction of the Battle of the Bulge in Germany's favor. Too many factors were working against the Nazis. Because of Allied air strength, German troop movements and supply shipments could take place only at night. More crucially, the German advance units were about to run out of fuel. One tank group was stalled within sight of the Meuse River, waiting for a shipment of gasoline that never came. Then, on January 3, 1945, the Allies launched an offensive of their own designed to cut the bulge of German-occupied territory in two.

By the eighth, the two Allied forces, one coming from the north, the other from the south, had drawn so close that Hitler was forced to authorize the withdrawal of German troops from the western half of the bulge. The Nazi tank groups that had roared west through the Ardennes a few weeks earlier, headed toward the Meuse and the port of Antwerp, were now rushing eastward in a desperate attempt to avoid being cut off. Not all of them made it. On January 16, the two Allied forces met a few miles from Bastogne, trapping more than 20,000 of the fleeing Germans. By then, the rest of the German Wehrmacht was slogging back toward the Fatherland on snow-covered roads and trails. The Battle of the Bulge, Hitler's last attempt to mount a major offensive, had ended in defeat.

As he abandoned Eagle's Nest and returned to Berlin, Hitler could not deny the reality of that defeat. "I know the war is lost," he confided to a close associate one night during an air raid. Sinking into depression, he muttered, "I'd like most of all to put a bullet through my head." But then he regained his determination. "We'll not capitulate. Never!" he said. "We may go down. But we'll take a world with us."

24 · DOWN TO THE BUNKER

As JANUARY WORE ON, it became harder and harder for Hitler to keep up his spirits. Wherever he looked, he saw nothing but setbacks. In the Far East, the Japanese had lost much of their fleet in a futile struggle to retain control of the Philippine Islands. In Italy, the Allies were moving steadily northward against a German army that was attempting to defend Mussolini's puppet government. And in eastern Europe, 3 million Soviet soldiers launched an offensive on a front extending from the Baltic Sea all the way down through Poland. The best the 750,000 German troops facing them could do was slow the pace of the Soviet advance wherever possible.

On January 17, 1945, the distant rumble of Soviet artillery could be heard at Auschwitz. The fearful camp guards rounded up 58,000 thinly clothed prisoners and marched them off to the west in a freezing wind for possible use as hostages. Many either fell dead along the way or were shot if they could not keep moving. When the Soviets finally reached Auschwitz on the twenty-seventh, they found almost 7,000 sick and starving inmates who had been left behind. Most of them were too weak to stand up and greet their liberators. Photographs of these survivors gave westerners their first painful glimpse of the horrors perpetrated in the camps.

Similar scenes of cruelty and death were revealed when the Allies liberated Dachau, Buchenwald, Bergen-Belsen, and other concentration camps in Germany. But they did not arrive soon enough to save the life of teenaged Anne Frank, who would become famous for her diary of the years she and her family spent hiding from the Germans in Nazi-occupied Holland. Anne died of typhus at Bergen-Belsen sometime in January 1945, a few months before the Allied soldiers got there.

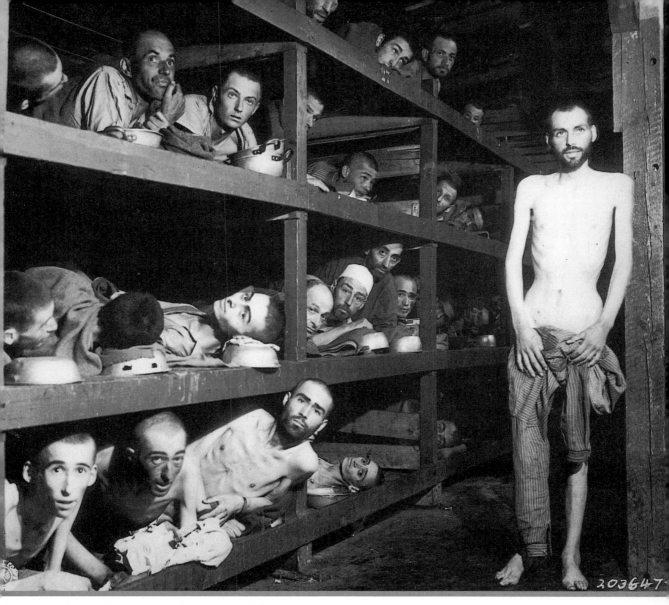

Starved prisoners, liberated by Allied troops, rest in their bunks in the Buchenwald concentration camp. *The National Archives*

Adolf Hitler made his last speech to the German people on January 30, the twelfth anniversary of his coming to power. He tried to rally the radio audience by saying, "However grave the crisis may be at the moment, it will, despite everything, finally be mastered by our unalterable will, by our readiness for sacrifice, and by our abilities." Even the bravest fighter's will needs to be backed up by weapons, however. And that day Albert Speer handed the Führer a memo stating that Germany's war plants would soon be unable to provide the necessary tanks, guns, and ammunition. Too many war factories had been destroyed in air raids or seized by the advancing Allied armies.

A furious Hitler ordered Speer not to show the memo to anyone else. Such predictions smacked of defeatism, he said. But the seriousness of the situation was brought forcibly home to the Führer on February 3, when a fleet of American bombers pounded Berlin in the heaviest raid of the war on the capital. Much of the city center was completely leveled, and Hitler's apartment in the Reich Chancellery was gutted by firebombs. He himself was forced to move down to the Führer Bunker, a two-story complex of underground rooms located deep below the Chancellery garden.

Originally constructed in 1936 for possible use as an air-raid shelter, the bunker had been deepened, enlarged, and reinforced in 1943. The complex was completely self-sufficient, with its own heating, lighting, ventilation, and water pumps, all run by a diesel generator. On the upper level were twelve small rooms surrounding a central chamber that served as the dining room. A curving flight of stairs led down to the lower level, where a reception room, a conference room, and the six-room suite reserved for Hitler and Eva Braun were located. No fresh air or natural light reached the bunker. Instead, ventilation fans whirred constantly, and artificial lighting gave the residents a pale, sickly look. Down in the bunker, it was hard to tell day from night.

To escape the harsh reality of his situation, Hitler spent hours studying a wooden model his architects had made for him. It showed in detail how his boyhood city of Linz, Austria, would look when it was rebuilt after the war. He also began to dictate his last will and testament to his chief aide, Martin Bormann. Unlike some famous men who repent of their sins and mistakes near the end of their lives, Hitler defiantly affirmed all his actions, including his campaign to eliminate Europe's Jews. "For us, this has been an essential process of disinfection, which we have prosecuted *to its ultimate limit*," he dictated, "and the world of the future will be eternally grateful to us."

Hitler nursed a secret hope that, as the Soviets advanced across Europe, the British and Americans would become increasingly alarmed. As a result, he thought they would want to negotiate a favorable peace with Germany in order to prevent a Soviet takeover. This hope was dashed in mid-February, when President Roosevelt, Prime Minister Churchill, and Premier Stalin met at the Black Sea resort city of Yalta in

British Prime Minister Winston Churchill, U.S. President Franklin D. Roosevelt, and Soviet Premier Joseph Stalin meet at Yalta in the Soviet Union in February 1945.
The National Archives

the Soviet Union to synchronize their military offensives and decide on the postwar division of Germany into four occupation zones. The fourth zone would be administered by the French. However, the Führer still believed the Allies' conflicting outlooks would split them and lead to a last-minute turnaround in the war.

Realistic or not, this belief was one of the things that kept Hitler going as word of fresh defeats on all fronts reached the bunker. In the west, the

U.S. and British troops prepare to cross the bridge over the Rhine River at Remagen, Germany, March 1945. *The National Archives*

Allies swept across one of the Rhine River bridges before the Germans could blow it up, establishing a firm foothold in Germany's industrial heartland. In the east, the Soviets had reached the Oder River and by mid-March were within 100 miles of Berlin. Despite the dangers involved, Hitler insisted on visiting the Oder front and meeting with the defenders. It would prove to be his last trip out of Berlin. To avoid notice, he was driven in a humble Volkswagen instead of his usual Mercedes.

At a castle on the Oder, the Führer pleaded with his army commanders to hold the Soviets back from the capital. He promised them that new secret weapons would be ready momentarily, and hinted at a bomb more destructive than even the rocket-driven V-2s, first deployed against England in November 1944. But this was only wishful thinking on the Führer's part. While the Americans were getting ready to test an atomic bomb in the spring of 1945, Germany's atomic weapons program was still at an early stage of development.

By the end of March, all German resistance in the Ruhr industrial region had ended, and the Allies were marching steadily across northern and central Germany. In the east, one Soviet army crossed the Oder while another occupied Vienna and moved toward southern Germany. Hitler was briefly overjoyed on April 12 when word reached the bunker that President Roosevelt had died. "Here, read this!" Hitler said to Albert Speer, handing him the news bulletin. "The war is not lost! Roosevelt is dead!" But his joy was short-lived. In the days that followed, there was no change in Allied military operations, and on April 17, more than 325,000 German troops, along with twenty generals, surrendered to the Americans.

Hitler's fifty-sixth birthday on April 20 was a cheerless affair. Unlike earlier years, when the entire nation had celebrated the Führer's birthday, this year the observance was limited to the bunker and the Chancellery garden. Hitler, stooped and shaky, slowly climbed the stairs to the garden in midafternoon to meet with twenty teenagers from the Hitler Youth who had displayed bravery in the defense of Berlin. He said a few words to the boys, patted several on the cheek, then returned to the safety of the bunker. He would not leave it again alive.

The Führer congratulates a twelve-year-old Hitler Youth soldier who had been awarded an Iron Cross for blowing up a Soviet tank with a hand grenade. This is one of the last known photos of Adolf Hitler. *AP Wide World Photos*

In late afternoon, word reached the Führer during his daily military briefing that the Soviets were now just sixty-five miles east of Berlin and advancing steadily. Only one road south from the city was still open, and the city's remaining airfields were under constant threat from Allied bombers. Many of Hitler's aides urged him to fly south to his retreat at Berchtesgaden while there was still time, but he refused. "I know what I want," he said. "I will fight on here in Berlin."

Other leaders were not so reluctant to leave the capital. Admiral Karl Dönitz traveled to north Germany at the Führer's request to take command of the armed forces stationed there. Albert Speer soon followed Dönitz. Himmler also went to the north, where he attempted to open peace negotiations with the Allies through a Swedish intermediary. The SS chief operated in secrecy, since he knew Hitler opposed any contact with the enemy. In the meantime, Göring had flown to southern Germany to direct what was left of the Luftwaffe from a base in the German Alps. Of those who had been closest to Hitler, only Goebbels and Bormann stayed on in Berlin as the Allies gradually closed in from all sides.

On April 22, the exploding shells from Soviet heavy artillery could be heard for the first time in the bunker. The Führer ordered one of his generals to assemble all remaining units in the area, including naval and Luftwaffe forces untrained in ground warfare, and launch a last-ditch counterattack on the Soviets. When he was told it couldn't be done, something seemed to snap in Hitler. He screamed that he had been betrayed by everyone he had trusted. The army had always been full of traitors, he said, and now even the SS was lying to him. No one was manning the antitank defenses, Luftwaffe pilots were afraid to fly, and the soldiers at the front had ceased to fight!

His audience of generals and aides quaked with fear as the Führer ranted on, then watched in stunned silence as he slumped into a chair and stared vacantly forward, his face drained of all color. Some who were present thought he had suffered a stroke. But then he spoke, in a low, whispery voice. "The war is lost," he said, startling those who had never before heard him admit even the possibility of defeat. "This is the end," he went on. "I shall remain here in Berlin, defending the city to the last. And then I shall shoot myself." It was a threat the Führer had first voiced back when the beer-hall putsch failed in 1923, but this time his listeners were sure that he meant it.

After telling his aides that they were free to leave Berlin if they wanted to, he summoned Eva Braun, his two secretaries, and his cook. He informed them of his plans, then told them to get ready to fly to south Germany within the hour. Eva was the first of the four to respond. She went up to Hitler and took both of his hands in hers. "You must know that I shall stay with you," she said. "I won't let you send me away." The other three echoed Eva, saying they wanted to stay with him also.

Hitler looked from one woman to another. "If only my generals were as brave as you are," he said with feeling. Then he did something no one had ever seen him do in public before: He kissed Eva on the lips.

After that, events moved swiftly. Hitler asked the Goebbels family to join him in the bunker, and the Propaganda Minister, the Führer's most devoted ally, arrived shortly thereafter. He was accompanied by his wife, Magda, and their six children, who ranged in age from four to twelve. Meanwhile, the situation in the world beyond the bunker worsened by the hour. Soviet troops completed a circle around Berlin on April 24, blocking the last main road from the capital to the west. That same day, the city's two remaining airports came under heavy Soviet artillery fire.

On April 25, Soviet troops coming from the east met American troops advancing from the west on the banks of the Elbe River near the central German town of Torgau. Hitler's Reich was now cut in two. On the same day, 318 Allied bombers mounted a massive raid on the Berghof, Hitler's mountain retreat at Berchtesgaden where he had spent so much time before and during the war. When the bombers were through with it, the Berghof had been reduced to a mass of twisted rubble. One side of the house had been completely demolished, and what was left of the tin roof dangled in midair.

At dawn on April 27, the Soviet army overran Berlin's last two airports. Now Hitler could not have left the city even if he had wanted to. That afternoon, his hand shaking, he managed to pin an Iron Cross on the coat of a small boy who had blown up a Russian tank. The boy was so tired that he dropped to the floor when he started to leave the bunker, and fell fast asleep there in the corridor. The Führer's aides did not disturb him.

In April 1945, Joseph and Magda Goebbels and their six children joined Hitler in the bunker. This photo, taken in happier times in 1935, shows the Goebbelses with their first three children. *AP Wide World Photos*

Hitler summoned one of his secretaries on the evening of April 28 and told her he wanted to dictate his personal will. She couldn't have been more startled by the Führer's opening words: "I have decided now, before the end of my earthly career, to take as my wife the woman who, after many years of loyal friendship, came of her own free will to this city, already almost besieged, in order to share my fate. At her request, she goes to her death with me as my wife."

Earlier, in a conversation with one of his aides, the Führer had expressed his fear of being captured alive. He had no intention, he said, of allowing Stalin to exhibit him in a cage and parade him through the streets of Moscow. Now, in dictating his will, he spelled out exactly what he wanted done. "My wife and I choose to die in order to escape the shame of overthrow or capitulation," he said. "It is our wish that our bodies be burned immediately, here at the Chancellery where I have performed the greater part of my daily work during the twelve years I served my people."

The wedding of Adolf Hitler and Eva Braun took place in the bunker conference room shortly before midnight on the twenty-eighth. Nine guests were present, including the Goebbelses and Martin Bormann. Eva wore an evening gown of black silk taffeta, and Hitler was dressed in his uniform. An official from a nearby military unit performed the ceremony. Afterward, Hitler took his bride by the arm and led the way to his study, where the wedding feast had been laid out. The guests ate sandwiches and drank champagne, and even the Führer sipped a little wine. But the guests' loud chatter and the dance music from a record player could not drown out the distant rumble of Russian artillery fire.

On the evening of the twenty-ninth, Hitler made plans for the final act in the drama. By then, all of Berlin's remaining supplies of ammunition, food, and other essentials were either in Russian hands or under attack. The Führer called the members of his inner circle to his study and handed out vials of cyanide, a deadly poison. They could take it, he said, if like him and his wife they wished to avoid capture by the Russians.

Goebbels reminded the Führer that the vials were two years old and wondered aloud if their contents were still effective. There was only one way to test that—try out the poison on a living creature. And the only possible subject for the test was Hitler's dog, Blondi. Hitler left the room while one of the doctors in the bunker forced the contents of a vial down the dog's throat. She died instantly. The Führer returned and glanced briefly at the animal who had been his loyal companion throughout the war years. Then, without saying anything, he went into his bedroom and shut the door.

That same evening Hitler learned of the terrible fate of his partner in the war, Benito Mussolini. The Italian dictator had fled the advancing Allied army with his mistress, Clara Petacci, only to be captured by resistance fighters near Lake Como in northern Italy. After debating the dictator's fate, his captors executed both Mussolini and Petacci. Their bodies were taken to the nearby city of Milan, where they were hung by the feet in a public square for all to see.

The news from Italy reinforced the decisions the Führer had already made about his own end. "I will not fall into the hands of the enemy, dead or alive!" he told his aides. "After I die, my body shall be burned and so remain undiscovered forever!" To make sure his last request could be carried out, his aides went in search of gasoline to fuel the cremation. The military garrison stationed next to the Chancellery had none to spare, so the aides tapped the only other available source: Under cover of darkness, they drained more than fifty gallons of gasoline from the tanks of wrecked cars parked near what was left of the Chancellery.

Early in the morning of April 30, Hitler received a report that the defenders of Berlin could not hold out against the Soviets for more than twenty-four hours. Later that morning, word came that one advance Soviet unit had fought its way into the street next to the bunker. Time had run out for the Führer. At half past three that afternoon, he and his wife went into his study together. Goebbels, Bormann, and his other close associates waited outside. No sounds were heard through the thick metal door, but after ten minutes the men opened it and entered the room.

Inside they found Hitler and Eva sitting next to one another on the small sofa. She was slumped to the Führer's left, and the bitter-almond smell of cyanide surrounded her body. Hitler had fallen forward over a low table. There was a bullet hole in his right temple, and his pistol—the same one he had carried since the 1920s—lay on the floor by his feet. At right angles to the sofa, atop a bureau, was one of the few personal items in the room: a picture of Hitler's mother as a young girl.

"The Chief is dead," Hitler's SS aide announced to those waiting for word outside the study. Then he and the Führer's other aides set to work to carry out his final wishes. They wrapped Hitler's and Eva's bodies in blankets and carried them up several flights of stairs to the bomb-scarred Chancellery garden. Ducking an almost constant rain of Soviet shells, they laid out the bodies side by side in a shallow depression and doused them with the gasoline they had collected earlier. Matches failed to ignite the fuel, but the men finally got a fire going with a torch made of paper. Then they scurried to the shelter of the bunker doorway, where they watched as a great ball of fire enveloped the bodies of the Führer and his bride. Later that night, the aides crept out to cover the smoking remains with a layer of earth.

Thus ended the life of Adolf Hitler. An extraordinary villain who promised to restore his nation's honor and dignity, but plunged it instead into a disastrous war. A man who professed to love art and culture, but who embarked on the most ruthless campaign of genocide the world had ever known. A leader who seized an empire extending from the Atlantic Ocean to the Volga River, but who, at the time of his death, was fighting to hold on to a few acres in the center of Berlin. Hitler was dead, but his closest associates were still alive, and the war he had started was not over yet.

Two Russian soldiers point to the spot in the Chancellery garden where the charred bodies of Hitler and Eva Braun were unearthed. In the center of the picture is one of the air vents that led down to the Führer's bunker. *The National Archives*

25 · HITLER LIVES

IT WASN'T LONG BEFORE another of the leading Nazis joined his Führer in death. On May 1, Joseph Goebbels and his wife climbed the bunker steps to the Chancellery garden and swallowed vials of poison. An aide then set their bodies ablaze.

Earlier that day, Magda Goebbels had watched as a doctor injected her six children with morphine; then she herself had placed crushed poison capsules in their mouths as they slept. "A world without Hitler and National Socialism is not worth living in," Mrs. Goebbels had told a relative a few days before. She was sure, she said, that "a merciful God will understand my sparing the children that sort of life."

Not all those in the bunker were so ready to give up their lives. Hitler's secretaries and aides formed six separate groups that fled at carefully spaced intervals on the evening of May 1. They followed an escape route through underground tunnels, hoping to elude capture by the Soviets. Many of them, including Hitler's youthful secretaries, survived to tell the story of his end. Before the last group left the bunker, they poured the remaining gasoline on the furniture in the conference room and set the Führer's final residence on fire. When the Soviets descended into the bunker the following day, the fires were still smoldering.

The final collapse of the Third Reich followed swiftly. Before his death, Hitler had appointed Admiral Dönitz his successor. Acting in that capacity, Dönitz on May 7 signed an unconditional surrender that called for all German troops to lay down their arms within twenty-four hours. Heinrich Himmler, who was still in northern Germany, decided to disguise himself in an attempt to avoid arrest. He shaved off his mustache, put a patch over one eye, and assumed a different name. But the British spotted him anyway and sent him to prison. Fearing that his role in the extermination of the Jews would be exposed, Himmler bit into a poison capsule concealed in his clothing and died instantly.

On May 8, 1945, all the Allied countries celebrated V-E Day—V-E stood for "Victory in Europe." The following day, Hermann Göring was arrested by American soldiers in southern Germany, and later in the month, the members of Admiral Dönitz's provisional government, including Albert Speer, were placed in custody also. Three months later, in August, the United States dropped its secret weapon, the atomic bomb, on the Japanese cities of Hiroshima and Nagasaki. Those devastating blasts stunned the world and were followed almost immediately by Japan's surrender. Now the world celebrated V-J Day—"Victory in Japan." The Second World War, which Adolf Hitler had triggered almost six years before when he invaded Poland—the war that had claimed at least 50 million lives—was finally over.

Two injured German teenage soldiers make their way to an Allied prisoner-of-war camp after the fighting ends. *The National Archives*

That same August, the four Allied powers established a special court at Nuremberg, the city where the Nazis had held their party congresses. The court would try twenty-two of Germany's former leaders for crimes against humanity. Among other things, the defendants were charged with the extermination of civilian populations, especially the Jews; the widespread use of slave labor; the looting of occupied countries; and the mistreatment and murder of prisoners of war. The trial opened in November 1945 and lasted ten months. During the course of it, a long parade of witnesses testified about the defendants' criminal actions. Films of the death camps were shown, some of them so grisly that spectators in the courtroom averted their eyes.

Nazi leaders in the dock at the Nuremberg trial. From left to right in the front row: Hermann Göring, Rudolf Hess, Foreign Minister Joachim von Ribbentrop, and Field Marshal Wilhelm Keitel. *The National Archives*

In the end, three of the defendants were acquitted. Eight others, including Albert Speer, received long prison sentences. One of the eight, Rudolf Hess, Hitler's close associate who had flown to Britain early in the war, was given a life sentence. The remaining eleven defendants were found guilty of all charges and were condemned to death by hanging. Only one of the latter, Hermann Göring, cheated his executioners. Two hours before he was to go to the gallows, the former commander of the Luftwaffe swallowed a cyanide capsule and died in his cell.

Several questions about the Nazi leaders remained unanswered after the Nuremberg trials. One mystery concerned the fate of Martin Bormann, the Führer's closest associate in his final days. Bormann was in one of the groups that fled the bunker after Hitler's suicide, and he had not been heard of since. Over the years, rumors spread that he had been sighted in Brazil, Argentina, or Paraguay, South American countries to which many former Nazis had gone. Only in 1973 was the mystery solved. Workers excavating a site near the ruins of the bunker came upon the remains of two men, one of whom was positively identified as Martin Bormann. His attempt to escape the burning bunker had not taken him very far.

Another mystery centered on the whereabouts of Adolf Eichmann, the SS officer who had organized the transportation of millions of Jews to death camps. Arrested by the Allies in the spring of 1945, he escaped and made his way to Argentina, where he built a new life under an assumed name. Israeli agents tracked him down in 1960 and managed to abduct him to Israel. There he was tried and hanged in 1962 for crimes against the Jewish people, and against humanity.

The biggest mystery concerned Adolf Hitler's remains. Many surviving eyewitnesses confirmed that he had died by his own hand in the bunker, but none of them were present when Russian troops unearthed his remains in the Chancellery courtyard. Consequently, rumors sprang up that Hitler and Eva Braun had somehow managed to escape from Berlin, and that doubles had died in their place. One report claimed that the Hitlers were living on a German-owned hacienda in Argentina, another that they had been spotted in Innsbruck, Austria.

The Soviets contributed to the confusion. Stalin's secret police were in charge of the investigation, and they did not choose to reveal what, if anything, they had found in the courtyard. Only in 1968, fifteen years after Stalin's death in 1953, did a Soviet journalist report that Hitler's jawbone and teeth had been identified. And it wasn't until 1995, after the cold war between the Western powers and the Soviet Union had ended, that the Russians disclosed that they had in their possession the remains of Hitler's skull, with a bullet hole in it. The skull had been shipped to Moscow soon after the end of the war and kept ever since in a government archive.

Hitler's earthly remains may finally have been laid to rest, but unfortunately his racist philosophy lives on. It has been given a name, neo-Nazism ("neo" means "new"), and those who practice it are known as neo-Nazis. Today, neo-Nazi groups can be found in many countries. They attract angry, frustrated individuals who feel society has left them behind and are looking for someone to blame—much as the young Adolf Hitler did when he was drifting aimlessly around Vienna and Munich in the years before World War I.

Neo-Nazis in Britain and elsewhere often shave their heads, which has led to their being called "skinheads." If they can obtain them, they wear SS insignia on their military-style clothing, and some have swastikas tattooed on their arms or skulls. They espouse Hitler's racial doctrines of white supremacy and hatred of the Jews, and they frequently engage in attacks upon immigrants. In Hungary, Slovakia, and the Czech Republic, neo-Nazi skinheads frequently attack gypsies; in France, they focus their hatred on North African immigrants.

The eastern part of Germany became a hotbed of neo-Nazism in the 1990s. After the Berlin Wall came down in 1989, the people living in East Germany, which had been a Communist country, rejoiced in their new freedom. But severe economic problems developed in the former East Germany following reunification with capitalist West Germany. The unemployment rate jumped to more than 20 percent, and with it came a sharp rise in neo-Nazi incidents. Roving bands of jobless, resentful skinheads staged attacks on Turkish and North African immigrants, and some of the victims died of their injuries.

The police chief of Dresden, a city in eastern Germany, offered an explanation: "We came from a Communist society where everything was laid out for you—youth groups, work groups, no decisions to make. And now you have young people coming into a void with often embittered parents behind them, and their disorientation turns to neo-Nazi violence."

German neo-Nazis march past the Brandenburg Gate in Berlin on March 12, 2000, the sixty-second anniversary of Hitler's annexation of Austria.
Associated Press AP

The neo-Nazi movement wasn't limited to European countries. Many groups also became active in the United States under such names as the Aryan Revolutionary Army, the National Association for the Advancement of White People, the World Church of the Creator, and the Aryan Nations. Exercising their free speech rights under the First Amendment to the Constitution, they spread lies about the threat of a worldwide

An Aryan Nations member raises his arm in the Nazi salute as he marches through the streets of Coeur d'Alene, Idaho, on July 18, 1998.
Associated Press AP

Jewish conspiracy that came straight out of the pages of *Mein Kampf*. They also denied that the Holocaust ever happened, despite overwhelming evidence to the contrary.

At the former Aryan Nations headquarters, located in the 1990s on a remote compound in Hayden Lake, Idaho, stained-glass swastikas decorated the windows of the church and a silver bust of Adolf Hitler stood next to the pulpit. Nazi flags flew over the guard tower. Taking his lead from the Führer, Richard Butler, founder of the Aryan Nations, preached that Aryans were God's chosen people, Jews were the offspring of the

Devil, and nonwhites were subhuman "mud creatures." His ultimate goal was to establish a "White American Bastion" in five Pacific Northwest states and secede from the "Jew-nited States of America."

Butler's plans for the Aryan Nations came to an abrupt halt in 2000. That year an Idaho court ruled in favor of a mother and son who charged that they had been stopped for no reason while driving past Butler's compound and brutally beaten by his security guards. The court forced Butler to pay heavy damages, and he lost the Hayden Lake compound as part of the settlement. Butler wasn't ready to give up on the Aryan Nations, however. While he looked for a new compound, he vowed to continue broadcasting his message via the Internet.

More than than 2,000 groups promoting anti-Semitism, white supremacy, homophobia, and anti-immigration policies have established web sites on the Internet. Adopting the propaganda techniques perfected by Joseph Goebbels, Hitler's Propaganda Minister, the creators of these neo-Nazi sites think nothing of spreading lies about their chosen targets. A good example is this message from the web site of the World Church of the Creator, which tries to find a way to blame the Jews for the 1999 high school shootings in Colorado, although there is absolutely no evidence to support the charges:

> The shootings on Adolf Hitler's birthday at the high school in Littleton, Colorado, should give us pause to reflect. . . . What we should reflect upon is how a society which was once clean and stable has, through the destructive influence of the Jew, caused yet another massacre of our White youth—this time by Jewish gunmen masquerading as believers in "Nazism" to the glee of a Jewish press which has conveniently failed to report the truth of their background.

Two other neo-Nazi organizations even had words of praise for the men who carried out the monstrous attacks on the World Trade Center and the Pentagon on September 11, 2001. On his web site, August Kreis, a spokesman for the Aryan Nations, had regularly denounced Israel and the Jews and supported what he called the "Islamic freedom fighters." In the wake of the attacks, Kreis stated that he felt an "ideological oneness" with the terrorists.

Billy Roper, a leader of another neo-Nazi organization, the National Alliance, went further than Kreis. In an e-mail sent to Alliance members, he wrote, "The enemy of our enemy [the Jews] is, for now at least, our friend. We may not want them [the terrorists] marrying our daughters, just as they would not want us marrying theirs. . . . But anyone willing to fly an airplane into a building to kill Jews is all right by me. I wish our members had half as much testicular fortitude."

Fortunately, the total membership of neo-Nazi hate groups in the United States has never been large. In the late 1990s, it was estimated that 25,000 men and women belonged to such organizations, and some 150,000 more were sympathizers. At the same time, other estimates claimed that approximately 70,000 skinheads were active in various European countries. But these figures did not include the thousands of people who occasionally attended gatherings of neo-Nazis, read their publications, visited their web sites, and were influenced to a greater or lesser degree by their ideas.

Could another Adolf Hitler rise to power and prominence from the neo-Nazi movement? At first glance, it seems unlikely; the groups in question are so small. But the Nazi Party was just as small and insignificant when Hitler joined it in the early 1920s. Much would depend on the political and economic conditions prevailing at the time. If a country experienced a sudden economic and spiritual collapse, as Germany did following World War I, and as the entire world did during the Great Depression of the 1930s, then a call might go out for a savior—a leader who could restore the country's pride and fiscal health and inspire new hope for the future in its despairing citizens. That was the call to which Adolf Hitler responded in 1933.

But even if drastic social conditions produced a new leader like Hitler, there's no reason the world should extend the same leeway to him that it did toward his predecessor. With the hindsight of history, it's clear that the Führer's rise to power could have been stopped, or at least braked, at many places along the way. If the moderate political parties in Germany had put aside their differences and joined forces against him, he might have been defeated at the polls in the crucial elections of the early 1930s. Later, if France and Britain had taken a strong stand, he might not have dared to reoccupy the Rhineland, or invade Austria and Czechoslovakia, or launch a Blitzkrieg attack on Poland.

Above all, if more of Germany's Jews—not to mention the religious and political leaders of other countries—had taken seriously what Hitler wrote in *Mein Kampf* when it first appeared, the worst effects of the Holocaust might have been lessened if not averted entirely. So many ifs. The trick will be to apply them *before* rather than *after* the fact, should another Hitler come to power in a time of crisis.

At the end of the political testament he dictated in the last days of his life, Adolf Hitler refused to accept the reality of Germany's defeat. Instead, he said the six-year war the country had waged would one day be recognized as "the most glorious and valiant manifestation of a nation's will to existence." Going further, he predicted that National Socialism would rise again, and that the sacrifices he and his soldiers had made in the struggle against "international Jewry" would be vindicated at last.

The challenge to the world's peoples couldn't be clearer. Now and in the future, every possible step must be taken to ensure that the Führer's final predictions never come true.

GLOSSARY OF GERMAN WORDS AND TERMS

Blitzkrieg—Lightning warfare. Often used to describe fast-moving attacks by tanks and planes.

Bund Deutscher Mädchen (BDM)—League of German Girls, the female counterpart of the Hitler Youth. For girls ages fourteen and up.

Führer—Leader; title assumed by Adolf Hitler as head of Nazi Germany, 1933–45.

Gestapo—Abbreviation for <u>Ge</u>heime <u>Staatspo</u>lizei, the Secret State Police, a bureau of the SS.

Hitlerjugend—Hitler Youth. A Nazi Party organization for young men ages fourteen and up.

Jungmädel—Young Girls. Official Nazi youth organization for girls of ten to fourteen. Affiliated with the *Bund Deutscher Mädchen*.

Jungvolk—Young People. Official youth organization for boys of ten to fourteen. It was linked to the *Hitlerjugend*.

Kristallnacht—Literally, Crystal Night, but usually called the Night of Broken Glass. Name given the night of November 10, 1938, when crowds rampaged through the streets of German cities, looting Jewish-owned shops and vandalizing synagogues.

Lebensraum—Living space. As Hitler used the word, it meant additional territory for Germany.

Luftwaffe—The German air force.

Nazi Party—Abbreviation for the pronunciation of *Nationalsozialistische Deutsche Arbeiter Partei* (NSDAP), National Socialist German Workers' Party.

Reich—Germany, or the German government.

Reichstag—Formerly the legislative assembly, or parliament, of Germany. Also the building in Berlin where it met.

SA—Abbreviation for *Sturmabteilung*, Storm Detachment. Members of the SA were often called Brownshirts (because of the brown shirts they wore) or storm troopers.

SD—Abbreviation for *Sicherheitsdienst*, the Security Service of the SS within Germany.

SS—Abbreviation for *Schutzstaffel*, Guard Squadron. There were four sections of the SS, and many different bureaus within the sections. Among the best known bureaus were the SD, the Security Service within Germany, and the Gestapo, the Secret State Police.

Third Reich—Name given the Fascist state under the Nazis that existed in Germany from 1933 to 1945.

Volkssturm—People's Militia. Many of its middle-aged members were pressed into active service at the end of the war.

Wehrmacht—The German armed forces: the army, navy, and air force.

SOURCE NOTES AND BIBLIOGRAPHY

FROM BOYHOOD ON, I've been fascinated by Adolf Hitler. I grew up during World War II and can remember my parents discussing the fall of France, the air war over Britain, and the struggle for Stalingrad. In the course of their conversations, Hitler's name came up again and again.

And not just in my parents' heated discussions. Adolf Hitler's name and face were everywhere—on recruiting posters for the armed forces, in ads urging people to buy war bonds ("Join the Fight against the Führer!"), and in movies, where he was usually seen raging at his generals or proclaiming that his Nazi regime would last forever. I had a yen to find out just who Hitler was and why he was doing all the terrible things he was accused of. Now, more than fifty years later, I've set out in search of answers to my youthful questions by writing this biography.

Research for the book centered on three adult biographies of Hitler, each of which has its own unique strengths. John Toland's *Adolf Hitler* (Garden City, NY: Doubleday, 1976) benefits greatly from the interviews Toland conducted in the early 1970s with many elderly Germans and others who had actually known and worked with Hitler.

Ian Kershaw's two-volume portrait, *Hitler: 1889–1936: Hubris* and *Hitler: 1936–1945: Nemesis* (both New York and London: W. W. Norton & Company, 1999 and 2000, respectively), is by far the longest and most detailed study of the tyrant. It is also the most up-to-date, since Kershaw was able to draw upon the complete diaries of Joseph Goebbels and previously secret Russian intelligence files on Hitler, both of which came to light only in the 1990s.

The third biography, Joachim C. Fest's *Hitler* (translated from the German by Richard and Clara Winston; San Diego, London, New York: Harcourt Brace Jovanovich, 1974), was one of the first complete studies of the dictator to be written by a German. Fest, a respected journalist, also had access to German writings not readily available to an outsider. For me, his book was especially valuable since I don't read German myself, and had to rely on translated material in my research.

Another essential resource was *Mein Kampf* (My Struggle), Adolf Hitler's well-known autobiographical work (translated from the German by Ralph Manheim; Boston and New York: Houghton Mifflin, 1943). I drew on it for expressions of Hitler's feelings as a youth and young man, and for his views on various social and political questions. But I did my best to check all his statements against other sources, because Hitler frequently altered or omitted the facts about a situation if they conflicted with his beliefs.

Helping me to get a better grasp of Hitler's personality, and the ways in which various psychologists and historians have interpreted it, were two thought-provoking books: *The Hitler of History* by John Lukacs (New York: Alfred A. Knopf, 1997) and *Explaining Hitler: The Search for the Origins of His Evil* by Ron Rosenbaum (New York: Random House, 1998).

William L. Shirer's classic work *The Rise and Fall of the Third Reich: A History of Nazi Germany* (New York: Simon & Schuster, 1960) offered a comprehensive overview of Nazi Germany from its beginnings to its final defeat. Even more illuminating, on a personal level, was Shirer's *Berlin Diary: The Journal of a Foreign Correspondent, 1934–1941* (New York: Alfred A. Knopf, 1941), covering the years when Shirer was stationed in Berlin.

For a thorough, succinct history of the Holocaust, I relied on Lucy S. Dawidowicz's *The War Against the Jews, 1933–1945* (New York: Holt, Rinehart and Winston, 1975). C. L. Sulzberger's *World War II* (New York: American Heritage Press, 1985) helped to give me a clear picture of the war on all fronts, and to see where Hitler's Germany fit into the overall pattern of events. Although dryly written, H. W. Koch's *The Hitler Youth: Origins and Development 1922–45* (New York: Barnes & Noble Books, 1996) showed me how Hitler and his aides attempted to mold Germany's children into model young Nazis.

Biographies and autobiographies of other Nazi leaders revealed much about the inner workings of the Hitler regime. These books included Albert Speer's *Inside the Third Reich: Memories* (translated from the German by Richard and Clara Winston; New York: Macmillan, 1970), the recollections of Hitler's favorite architect and later the official in charge of Germany's war production; a biography of Speer that presents him in a less favorable light, *The Good Nazi: The Life and Lies of Albert Speer* by Dan van der Vat (Boston and New York: Houghton Mifflin, 1997); and Ralf Georg Reuth's *Goebbels* (translated from the German by Krishna Winston; New York, San Diego, London: Harcourt Brace, 1993), an incisive portrait of Hitler's Propaganda Minister.

Insights into German cultural life in the Nazi era came from *A Memoir: Leni Riefenstahl* (New York: St. Martin's Press, 1993), the autobiography of the gifted and controversial filmmaker, and from David Stewart Hull's comprehensive study *Film in the Third Reich: A Study of the German Cinema, 1933–1945* (Berkeley: The University of California Press, 1969).

I got a chilling insiders' view of the mass killings of Jews in eastern Europe from *"The Good Old Days": The Holocaust as Seen by Its Perpetrators and Bystanders* (edited by Ernst Klee, Willi Dressen, and Volker Riess; translated by Deborah Burnstone; New York: Konecky & Konecky, 1991). And Ada Petrova and Peter Watson's *The Death of Hitler: The Full Story with New Evidence from Secret Russian Archives* (New York and London: W. W. Norton, 1995) gave me the information I needed in order to write about Hitler's final hours and the disposal of his remains.

Source Notes by Chapter

(Topics appear in the order they are discussed within the chapter.)

CHAPTER 1. Origins of the concept of a dictator: *Encyclopedia Britannica, Columbia Encyclopedia.*

CHAPTER 2. Hitler's childhood and youth: Toland, Kershaw, Fest, *Mein Kampf.* August Kubizek's memories of Hitler: from Kubizek's book *The Young Hitler I Knew* (Boston: Houghton Mifflin, 1955), as excerpted by Toland. Dr. Edward Bloch's impressions of Hitler: from Bloch's article "My Patient Hitler" in *Collier's Magazine,* March 15 and 22, 1941, as recounted by Toland.

CHAPTER 3. Hitler in Vienna: Toland, Kershaw, Fest, *Mein Kampf.* Hitler's joy at being accepted for enlistment in the German army: *Mein Kampf.*

CHAPTER 4. Excerpts from Hitler's frontline letter to a friend: the Bundesarchiv (German Federal Archive), Koblenz, as excerpted by Toland. Hitler's army experiences during World War I: Toland, Kershaw, Fest, *Mein Kampf.* Hitler's impressions of Berlin and of the Jews in wartime Munich, and his reactions when blinded by mustard gas: *Mein Kampf.*

CHAPTER 5. Hitler's reaction to the news of Germany's defeat: *Mein Kampf.* His experiences in postwar Munich: Toland, Kershaw, Fest. Hans Frank's impression of Hitler: from Frank's memoirs, *Im Angesicht des Galgens* (Munich: Beck, 1953), as excerpted by Toland.

CHAPTER 6. History of the swastika: Toland; "A Symbol of Hatred Pleads Not Guilty," article in *The New York Times* by Sarah Boxer, June 12, 1999. The rise of the Nazi Party and Hitler's growing power within it: Toland, Kershaw, Fest. Hermann Göring's first impression of Hitler: from an unpublished entry in G. M. Gilbert's Nuremberg diary, as quoted by Toland. Ernst and Helene Hanfstaengl's initial impressions of Hitler: from interviews conducted by Toland with both Hanfstaengls, and from Helene's unpublished *Notes*. Hitler's speech before the beer-hall crowd: from the recollections of Professor Karl von Müller and Ernst Hanfstaengl, as recounted by Toland.

CHAPTER 7. The beer-hall putsch: Toland, Kershaw, Fest. Helene Hanfstaengl's conversations with Hitler: Toland's interview with Hanfstaengl and her unpublished *Notes*.

CHAPTER 8. Hitler's trial and incarceration in Landsberg Prison: Toland, Kershaw, Fest. Attempts to explain Hitler's deep-seated hatred of the Jews: Lukacs, Rosenbaum. Hitler's return to Party leadership: Toland, Kershaw, Fest, *Mein Kampf*. Joseph Goebbels's impressions of Hitler: *The Early Goebbels Diaries, 1925–1926* (London: Weidenfeld and Nicholson, 1962), as excerpted by Toland. Albert Speer's early admiration of Hitler: Speer. Impressions of Angela (Geli) Raubal, Hitler's niece: Interviews with Ernst and Helene Hanfstaengl, as reported by Toland. First meeting of Hitler and Eva Braun: from *Eva Braun: Hitler's Mistress* by Nerin Gun (New York: Meredith, 1968) as excerpted by Toland.

CHAPTER 9. The Nazi Party's electoral success: Toland, Kershaw, Fest. Hitler's relationship with Geli Raubal and her death: Kershaw, Fest, Toland, including material the latter gathered from an interview with Ilse Hess, Rudolf Hess's wife, and from photographer Heinrich Hoffman's reminiscences, *Hitler Was My Friend* (London: Burke, 1955). Hitler's remark about eating meat: from G. M. Gilbert's *The Psychology of Dictatorship* (New York: Ronald Press, 1950), as quoted by Toland.

CHAPTER 10. Hitler's campaign tactics in the election of 1932: Toland, Kershaw, Fest. The French ambassador's reaction to Hitler's victory parade: from André François-Poncet's *The Fateful Years: Memoris of a French Ambassador in Berlin, 1931–1938* (London: Gollancz, 1949), as quoted by Toland.

CHAPTER 11. The Reichstag fire: Toland, Kershaw, Fest. Actions against the Jews in 1933: Toland, Kershaw, Dawidowicz. The burning of "subversive" books and Goebbels's role in it: Reuth. Elimination of other German political parties and agreement with the Roman Catholic Church: Toland, Kershaw, Fest.

CHAPTER 12. The Röhm purge: Toland, Kershaw, Fest. Hitler's last visit to Hindenburg: from Ernst Hanfstaengl's *The Missing Years* (London: Eyre and Spottiswoode, 1957), as quoted by Toland. The Nazi Party congress of 1934 and the film *Triumph of the Will*: Toland, Kershaw, Speer, Riefenstahl, Hull, and the author's own viewing of the film.

CHAPTER 13. Daily life in Hitler's Germany: Shirer's *Berlin Diary*. Better factory conditions: Toland. The German film industry under Goebbels's supervision: Hull. Formation of Nazi youth groups: Toland, Koch. Hitler's anti-Semitic views and acts: *Mein Kampf*, Toland. The Berlin Olympic Games of 1936: Toland, Anne Morrow Lindbergh's *The Flower and the Nettle: Diaries and Letters 1936–1939* (New York and San Diego: Harcourt Brace Jovanovich, 1976). Hitler's views of African American athletes: Speer.

CHAPTER 14. Hitler's thoughts on how far he can go: from *Es Spricht der Führer* (edited by Hildegard von Kotze and Helmut Krausnick; Gütersloh: S. Mohn, 1966), as quoted by Toland. The reoccupation of the Rhineland: Toland, Kershaw, Fest. Hitler's support of Franco in the Spanish Civil War: Toland, Kershaw, Fest. The Hanfstaengls' falling-out with Hitler: from Ernst Hanfstaengl's unpublished memoirs, as excerpted by Toland. Hitler's faith in his new physician, Dr. Theo Morell: from an interview conducted by Toland with another of Hitler's doctors, Erwin Giesing. The German-American Bund and the British Union of Fascists: Toland. Germany's need for more territory: Toland, Kershaw, Fest.

CHAPTER 15. Annexation of Austria: Toland, Kershaw, Fest. Reunion with boyhood friend August Kubizek: Kubizek, as excerpted by Toland.

CHAPTER 16. Germany's absorption of the Sudetenland: Toland, Kershaw, Fest. Hitler's unrelenting demands and Prime Minister Chamberlain's urgent attempts to get him to change his mind: from the unpublished memoirs of one of Hitler's aides, Captain Fritz Wiedemann, as reported by Toland. The plot to remove Hitler from power: Toland. Hitler's reactions after the Munich conference: Shirer's *Berlin Diary*. Churchill's quote about the Munich agreement:

Roger Parkinson's *Peace for Our Time: Munich to Dunkirk—The Inside Story* (New York: McKay, 1972), as repeated by Toland.

CHAPTER 17. *Kristallnacht:* Toland, Kershaw, Fest, Dawidowicz. Hitler's January 1939 speech on the "Jewish Question": *The Speeches of Adolf Hitler, April 1922–August 1939*, edited by Norman H. Baynes (New York: Oxford University Press, 1942), as excerpted by Toland. Germany's takeover of the rest of Czechoslovakia: Toland, Kershaw, Fest. Children's song in celebration of Hitler's fiftieth birthday: Toland. The Nazi-Soviet Nonaggression Pact: Toland, Kershaw, Fest. Plans for the invasion of Poland: Toland, Kershaw, Fest.

CHAPTER 18. The swift defeat of Poland: Toland, Kershaw, Fest, Sulzberger. The crowding of Jews into Polish ghettos and the building of more concentration camps: Dawidowicz. The German seizure of Norway, Denmark, the Low Countries, and France: Toland, Kershaw, Fest, Sulzberger. Hitler quotes upon seeing Paris: interview conducted by Toland with architect Hermann Giesler, who accompanied Hitler on the sightseeing tour.

CHAPTER 19. Winston Churchill's defiant speech of July 14, 1940: Churchill's *Blood, Sweat, and Tears* (New York: G. P. Putnam's Sons, 1941), as excerpted by Fest. The air campaign against Britain: Toland, Kershaw, Fest, Sulzberger. British retaliatory raid on Berlin: Shirer's *Berlin Diary*. Plans for an attack on the Soviet Union: Toland, Kershaw, Fest. Invasion of Yugoslavia and Greece: Toland, Kershaw, Fest, Sulzberger. Rudolf Hess's flight to Great Britain: Toland. Hitler's reactions to Hess's flight: postwar interrogations of Albert Speer and an account by Hitler aide Paul Schmidt, as reported by Toland.

CHAPTER 20. The invasion of the Soviet Union: Toland, Kershaw, Fest (Hitler's quotes regarding the campaign come from notes taken by two adjutants at Hitler's frontline headquarters, Werner Koeppen and Heinrich Heim, as excerpted by Toland). The Wannsee Conference and the first stages of the "Final Solution": Toland, Kershaw, Fest, Dawidowicz. Rommel's North African campaign: Sulzberger, Toland.

CHAPTER 21. The struggle for Stalingrad: Toland, Kershaw, Fest, Sulzberger. Hitler's angry outburst upon learning that General Paulus had surrendered: from *Hitlers Lagebesprechungen* (edited by Helmut Heiber; Stuttgart: Deutsche Verlag-Anstatt, 1962), as excerpted by Fest. Hitler's daily routines at Berchtesgaden: from interviews conducted by Toland with Gertraud (Traudl) Junge,

Hitler's private secretary from 1943 to 1945, and from Junge's unpublished memoirs, as excerpted by Toland. Downfall of Benito Mussolini and his rescue by Hitler: Toland, Kershaw, Sulzberger. The killing of more and more Jews: Toland, Kershaw, Fest, Dawidowicz. Himmler's speeches outlining the policy of extermination: from *Heinrich Himmler: Geheimreden 1933 bis 1945 und Andere Ansprachen,* edited by Bradley F. Smith and Agnes F. Peterson (Frankfurt am Main: Propyläen, 1974), as excerpted by Toland and Kershaw. The German military situation at the end of 1943: Toland.

CHAPTER 22. The White Rose group: Kershaw, Koch. The Allied invasion of France and Hitler's response: Toland, Kershaw, Sulzberger. The Stauffenberg plot to assassinate Hitler: Toland, Kershaw, Fest. Hitler's joyful reaction at having survived the blast: from Traudl Junge's unpublished memoirs, as excerpted by Toland. Hitler's radio address to the German people about the bomb plot: from *Reden und Proklamationen 1932–1945: Hitler,* edited by Max Domarus (2 vols., Wurzburg: Schmidt, 1962–63), as excerpted by Fest.

CHAPTER 23. The state of Hitler's health: Toland, Kershaw, Traudl Junge's memoirs. The fate of the army officers involved in the plot against Hitler, and Field Marshal Erwin Rommel's suicide: Toland, Kershaw, Fest. German setbacks in the west and east as the Allies close in: Toland, Sulzberger. The Battle of the Bulge: Toland, Kershaw, Fest, Sulzberger. Hitler's speech to the commanders of the Battle of the Bulge, urging them to hold on: from Heiber, as excerpted by Fest. Hitler's recognition of defeat but his determination to go on: from Nicolaus von Below's *Als Hitlers Adjutant, 1937–1945* (Mainz: Hase & Koehles, 1980), as recounted by Kershaw.

CHAPTER 24. State of the war in January 1945: Sulzberger. Liberation of Auschwitz: Toland. Death of Anne Frank: *Columbia Encyclopedia.* Hitler's move to the bunker: Fest, Toland, Kershaw. Layout of the bunker: Kershaw. Hitler's dictation of his last will and testament to Bormann: Toland. The Yalta Conference: Sulzberger. Hitler's glee at hearing of Roosevelt's death: Speer. Hitler's fifty-sixth birthday: Toland, Kershaw. Hitler's collapse as the Soviet army approaches the bunker: Toland, Kershaw, Fest. Eva Braun's vow to stay in Berlin with Hitler: from Traudl Junge's memoirs, as excerpted by Toland. The Allied armies draw the noose tighter: Toland, Kershaw, Fest, Sulzberger. Hitler's personal will and his marriage to Eva Braun: from Traudl Junge's memoirs, as excerpted by Toland. Hitler's final instructions to his aides about his death and burial: from interviews conducted by Toland with two of the aides,

Otto Gunsche and Erich Kempka. The deaths of Hitler and Eva Braun: Kershaw, Fest, Traudl Junge's memoirs, and interviews conducted by Toland with Gunsche and Kempka.

CHAPTER 25. The deaths of the Goebbels children: Toland, Kershaw, Fest, Petrova and Watson. Escape of staff members from the bunker: Toland, Kershaw. The end of the war: Sulzberger. The Nuremberg trials: Toland, Kershaw, Sulzberger. The fate of Martin Bormann: Kershaw. The mystery surrounding Hitler's remains: Petrova and Watson. Neo-Nazism in Germany today: News articles by Roger Cohen in *The New York Times*, February 28, 1999, August 21, 2000, and August 26, 2000. Neo-Nazism in the United States, and the activities of Richard Butler's organization, Aryan Nations: Article "Aryan Nations in the Dock," *Newsweek,* September 4, 2000; article "New Future for Aryan Nations Compound," *The New York Times,* March 7, 2001. Neo-Nazi sites on the Internet: article "Mainstream Sites Serve as Portals to Hate," *The New York Times,* November 30, 2000. World Church of the Creator message about the high school shootings in Littleton, Colorado: Newsletter of the Anti-Defamation League, 1999. Quotes from neo-Nazi web site and e-mail about the terrorist attacks on the World Trade Center and the Pentagon: article "Neo-Nazi Americans Hail the Butchers," *New York Post,* October 3, 2001.

Pages in *bold italic* type refer to illustrations.

21.00

--   Giblin, James.
B
Hitler   The life and death of
G   Adolf Hitler.

DATE			